THE PRESSED
MELODEON

THE PRESSED MELODEON

Essays on Modern Irish Writing

Ben Howard

Story Line Press   *1996*

Story Line Press, Three Oaks Farm, Brownsville, OR 97327

This publication was made possible thanks in part to the generous support of the Nicholas Roerich Museum, the Andrew W. Mellon Foundation, the National Endowment for the Arts, and our individual contributors.

Book design by Chiquita Babb

Five of the essays in this collection first appeared in the *Sewanee Review*: "Selective Laurels" (v. XCV, no. 3, Summer, 1987); "After the Coronachs" (v. XCVII, no. 1, Winter, 1989); "In the Shadow of the Gasworks" (v. XCIX, no. 1, Winter, 1991); "Seán O'Faoláin" (v. C, no. 2, Spring, 1992); and "Gael and Gall" (v. CI, no. 1, Winter, 1993). Two essays first appeared in *The Iowa Review*: "Angel in Clay" (v. 16, no. 2, Spring-Summer, 1986); and "Lyric Memory" (v. 18, no. 1, Winter, 1988). Two essays first appeared in *Prairie Schooner* and are reprinted by permission of the University of Nebraska Press: "Home from Home" (v. 60, no. 3, Fall, 1986); and "Articulating the Silences" (v. 67, no. 1, Spring, 1993). "The Pressed Melodeon" first appeared in *The Kenyon Review* (v. IX, no. 1, Winter, 1987).

Library of Congress Cataloging-in-Publication Data
Howard, Ben.
    The pressed melodeon : essays on modern Irish writing / Ben
Howard.
        p. cm.
    ISBN 1-885266-24-3
    1. English literature—Irish authors—History and criticism.
2. English literature—20th century—History and criticism.
3. Ireland—Intellectual life—20th century. 4. Ireland—In
literature. I. Title.
PR8753.H59 1996
820.9'9415—dc20   96-3711
                                               CIP

Acknowledgments

FOR ENCOURAGEMENT in the writing of these essays, as well as for their editing and publications, I am indebted to George Core, editor of the *Sewanee Review*; Hilda Raz, editor of *Prairie Schooner*; David Hamilton, editor of *The Iowa Review*; and Philip Church, former editor of the *Kenyon Review*.

For their insights and perspectives I am grateful to Eavan Boland, Philip Booth, Hayden Carruth, Michael Davitt, Catherine Delaney, Greg Delanty, Denis Donoghue, Robert Garratt, Dana Gioia, Eamon Grennan, Donald Hall, Seamus Heaney, Michael Heffernan, Patricia Holder, Earl Ingersoll, Dillon Johnston, Thomas and Eleanor Kinsella, Sara MacNeil, Derek Mahon, Robert McDowell, John Montague, Paul Muldoon, Howard Nemerov, Michael Stephens, Eamonn Wall, and Mervyn Wall. Thanks also to Carol Burdick, Pamela Lakin, and Heather Yanda for editorial assistance and to the NEH Steering Committee of Alfred University for financial support.

Some of these essays were written at the Tyrone Guthrie Center (Annaghmakerrig) in Co. Monaghan, Ireland. Others had their origin there. My thanks to Bernard and Mary Loughlin for their gracious hospitality.

For my son,
Alexander

Contents

Preface

"LOOKING BACK now at 1920-50," wrote Seán O'Faoláin in *The Irish* (1969), "my most profound regret is that it had not been possible for us all to have read cold Joyce in our warm teens. For after Yeats this green corner of the universe refused any longer to play Romantic ball. Ireland ceased to be a romantic island. We had needed the colder guide."

In O'Faoláin's reflection there is irony as well as pathos. Idealistic in his youth, he became himself that colder guide. And what he longed for in retrospect is what he and other Irish realists had labored for decades to provide. From the time of George Bernard Shaw to the present day, Irish writers have endeavored to discover the "real Ireland" behind the sentimental stereotypes, the warring ideologies, the outworn pieties and outright shams. That the veils of illusion have been partially the creation of Irish writers only complicates the project. "However they might think of themselves," observed O'Faoláin, "and many thought themselves tough realists . . ." the writers of his generation remained "*au fond* incurably local and romantic."

The essays collected in this volume focus primarily on Irish writing of the postwar period. Written for American literary journals, they deal with writers of the generations after O'Faolain's— writers for whom the old romanticism has been both a dwindling legacy and a living burden. In sensibilities as diverse as those of Seamus Heaney and Eavan Boland, John McGahern and Mary Beckett, Medbh McGuckian and Paul Muldoon, the enduring presence of Irish traditions—romantic and otherwise—has provoked responses ranging from reverential evocation to aggressive revision to "postmodern" pastiche. To clarify those responses, to illuminate them, and to provide the perspective of a sympathetic outsider have been my chief objectives. Although I doubt that Samuel Johnson's "common reader" ever existed, or exists today, my imagined audience has been the general, North American reader with an interest in Irish literature and at least a passing interest in modern Irish history.

During the ten-year period which these essays span, the Irish literary scene has continued to evolve. Ten years ago, the most talked-about Irish writers were the poets of Northern Ireland, and much of the energy came from the North. Since then, other literary communities have become more visible and influential, most notably those of Galway, Cork, and Dublin. Only this summer, Cork University Press published *Jumping Off Shadows*, a bilingual anthology of poems written by graduates of University College, Cork. Vibrant and iconoclastic, the book is also a reminder of that city's rich literary tradition.

Concurrent with the distribution of literary influence has been the dramatic emergence of Irish women writers, who have challenged the hierarchies and altered the complexion of Irish writing. "In previous centuries," writes Eavan Boland in *Object Lessons* (1995), "when the poet's life was an emblem for the grace and power of a society, a woman's life was often the object of his expression. . . By an ironic reversal, now that a woman's life is that emblem of grace and power, the democratization of our communities, of which her emergence is one aspect, makes a poet's life look suspect, can make it appear, to a wider society, elite and irrelevant. . ." Although in my judgment Boland overstates her case, it is not without foundation. Her book itself is a sign of the times, as are the success of the Salmon Poetry series in Galway and the Attic Press in Dublin, which have brought women's issues and younger women writers to national attention.

In view of the changes occurring in my subject, I have been tempted more than once to revise these essays. With hindsight I would change my emphases in many places. I would attempt to fill in the gaps. But apart from minor corrections, I have chosen not to revise these essays for book publication. As Allen Tate once remarked, a writer is someone who grows up in public, and that has certainly been true in the writing of these essays. Rather than refashion them, I would prefer to let them stand, both as essays in the etymological sense and as a chronicle of my encounters with Irish literary culture.

August 1995   *Ben Howard*

The Pressed Melodeon

Ten years ago Seamus Heaney read his poems at a poetry festival in Cambridge, England. His audience was largely British, but it also included Robert Duncan, Robert Creeley, Fielding Dawson, and other American writers. The atmosphere was congenial but unexpectedly tense. In his kindly, disarming manner, Heaney had made a few ironic remarks about Anglo-Irish relations, and several Cambridge students had angrily stomped out. As Heaney turned gingerly from the subject of British colonialism to his poems on Irish history, he nodded playfully to his American colleagues. "You see," he remarked to Duncan and Creeley, "you've had the frontier. We've had the bog."

Heaney's remark has stayed with me for a decade, perhaps because it reveals a special affinity between Irish and American poets, while also drawing a bold line between the two cultures. I have no Irish heritage, but I have lived in Ireland, and over the years I have been drawn to the poems of Patrick Kavanagh, Thomas Kinsella, John Montague, Richard Murphy, Derek Mahon, and other Irish poets of the generations after Yeats. Many things might explain this interest, not the least being the natural eloquence of Irish writers, the gift of fluency so evident in Montague and Heaney. But I suspect that the strongest attraction is the one Heaney's comment brings into focus—the historical capaciousness of Irish poetry, its power to contain and transform its melancholy past. Irish history being what it is, the historical imagination of the Irish poet often nurtures a sense of the tragic. And that in turn gives rise—in Kavanagh, in Paul Muldoon—to a gaiety of spirit, an antic redemptive vision. It would be unjust to say that such qualities are lacking in American poetry, but they are often in short supply, and to read Heaney's "Viking Dublin," or Montague's *The Rough Field*, or Mahon's "Derry Morning" is to satisfy a persistent hunger. It is, one might say, a hunger for images of the self in history, of personal identity in relation to historical process.

Of course, it does not take an American reader long to realize that the strange otherness of Irish poetry, its fascination with relics and regional histories and place-names, is matched by a strange likeness, a peculiar affinity. The poetry of the bog, as it turns out, and the poetry of the frontier have more in common than meets the eye. And the feeling some Americans have in visiting Ireland, the feeling of being at home in a foreign land, is re-created in reading the poems of Heaney or Michael Longley or Austin Clarke. It is as if our themes and obsessions—our troubled relations with language, our sense of discontinuity and disloca-tion, our fractures of identity—were being played out in a new and often more urgent context. What is for us a personal matter is often, for the Irish poet, a public and political matter, a question of tribal loyalty or partisan commitment.

Take, to begin with, the question of choosing—or creating—an authentic voice. In American poetry the plain style has been in vogue for twenty years or more, but lately poets as diverse as William Matthews, Robert Pinsky, and Judith Moffett have been prospecting for a richer, more formal, more musical vein of speech. In Ireland, the current has been flowing in the opposite direction, and younger poets have been divesting themselves of the grand manner of Yeats, while cultivating the demotic idiom of Patrick Kavanagh. But whatever the trend or fashion, the situation is more complicated for the Irish poet, who must choose not only between levels of diction but also between two languages, two cultures, two allegiances. To choose, as most have done, to write in English is to part company with the tradition of the bardic poets and with the language of most Irish poetry before the nineteenth century. But to choose, as Michael Hartnett, Nuala ní Dhomhnaill, and others have done, to write only in Irish is to make oneself an exile in a dying tongue. "Irish literature in English," John Montague notes, "is in the uneasy position that the larger part of its past lies in another language."[1] And, as Denis Donoghue observes, in Ireland the language of one's verse may be one thing, the language of the heart another:

> Irish writers find it peculiarly difficult to know what they are doing; they live upon a fractured rather than an integral tradition; they do not know which voice is to be trusted. Most of them speak English, but they have a sense, just barely acknowledged, that the true voice of feeling speaks in Irish, not a dead language like Latin but a banished language, a voice in exile. English, Irish: Protestant, Catholic: Anglo-Irish, Gael: in Ireland today we do not know what to do with these fractures.[2]

Nor does an American visitor know what to do with such fractures, or how to measure their depth and breadth. A young sculptor from County Galway told me that in her childhood she would have been ostracized for speaking English, or even for calling her native language "Gaelic," the English name. Yet her own speech was a rich mixture of English words and Irish rhythms, Dublin dialect and Irish expletives. Were her English words betrayals? Her Irish phrases a gesture to a faded cause?

John Montague, who was born in Brooklyn and grew up in County Tyrone, has caught the essence of the dilemma in a poem

---

[1] John Montague, ed., "In the Irish Grain," in *The Book of Irish Verse* (New York: Macmillan Co., 1983), pp. 21–22.

[2] Denis Donoghue, "Being Irish Together," *The Sewanee Review*, 84, No. 1, Winter, 1976, pp. 129–133.

about Irish schooling. Since the founding of the Irish Free State (later Éire, or the Republic of Ireland) in 1922, the Irish language has been compulsory in public and private schools. A banished language, it has become an imposed tongue, an entrée to the civil service—and a bane to Irish schoolchildren. Yet, as Montague's poem "A Grafted Tongue" makes clear, the situation was exactly the reverse in the mid-nineteenth century:

> An Irish
> child weeps at school
> repeating its English.
> After each mistake
>
> The master
> gouges another mark
> on the tally stick
> hung about its neck
>
> Like a bell
> on a cow, a hobble
> on a straying goat.
> To slur and stumble
>
> In shame
> the altered syllables
> of your own name;
> to stray sadly home
>
> And find
> the turf cured width
> of your parents' hearth
> growing slowly alien . . .
>
> Decades later,
> that child's grandchild's
> speech stumbles over lost
> syllables of an old order.

Montague published this poem in the early seventies. Its pessimism may now be somewhat out of date, given the growth of interest in the Irish language among the urban and professional classes. Cullen Murphy suggests that the Irish language has suffered "the fate of Morocco's Atlas lions, which are now extinct in the wild even as they propagate in captivity."[3] In Murphy's analogy, captivity equals Dublin and its environs, where a kind of "urban Gaeltacht" has been evolving. Montague makes a similar point in a recent interview, where he distinguishes between the Irish spoken on the seacoast and "school Irish mixed in with the older tongue." The older tongue is dying, but the new Irish is flourishing in the poetry of Gabriel Rosenstock, Michael Davitt, and other younger Irish poets. In Montague's opinion, Irish writing in the Irish language "has not been as healthy any time since the War."

Healthy or not, the native language haunts recent Irish poetry, whether the poet chooses to write in it or not. Gaelic words pepper the lines of Pearse Hutchinson, Paul Muldoon, and other English-speaking poets, and Irish place-names are often the loci of feeling. In "Anahorish," Seamus Heaney eulogizes his native landscape by recalling its name's original meaning: *anach fhíor uisce*: "place of clear water." He also compares the world's phonemes to the contours of the land:

> *Anahorish*, soft gradient
> of consonant, vowel-meadow,
>
> after-image of lamps
> swung through the yards
> on winter evenings.

The roots of feeling mingle with the roots of language. The "grafted tongue" appears extraneous, even in an English-speaking poet.

---

[3]Cullen Murphy, "The Irish Question," *The Atlantic Monthly*, 256, No. 3, September, 1985.

John Montague also meditates on place-names, but his mood is usually one of historical lamentation. In *The Dead Kingdom*, his book-length poem, he narrates a journey northward from Cork to his homeland in County Tyrone. The speaker is on a melancholy errand—a return for his mother's funeral. Along the way, he passes through decaying villages and towns, whose desolation mirrors his mood:

> and we leave, waving
> a plume of black smoke
> over the rushy meadows,
> small hills and hidden villages—
> Beragh, Carrickmore,
>
> Pomeroy, Fintona—
> place names that sigh
> like a pressed melodeon
> across this forgotten
> Northern landscape.

What Montague laments is both the places named and the names themselves. The sigh of the melodeon—a homely, parochial instrument—expresses exhaustion as well as sorrow.

It also expresses an outsider's yearning, an exile's bitter cry. Montague has identified the "intellectual exile's longing for home" as one of the "great Hibernian themes," uniting the travails of mad Sweeney with the alienation of modern Irish poets, himself included. Among recent Irish poets there are no political exiles, but Montague, Heaney, Mahon, and others continue to explore the theme, whatever their actual circumstances. Some, like ni Dhomhnaill, write in "a banished language, a voice in exile." Others, like Heaney and Kinsella, divide their time between Ireland and America, joining an insider's knowledge with an outsider's detachment. But, whatever form it might take, the Irish poet's sense of exile has a sharp-edged, parochial definition. It means estrangement from a particular parish. Its pain has local origins.

Of course, it might be argued that exile *always* has a local habitation and a name, and that may well be true for many European writers-in-exile, such as Czeslaw Milosz. But I believe it is not true for those postwar American poets who have explored the themes of homelessness and dislocation. Among the older generation there are some, like William Stafford and James Wright, who have linked their sense of estrangement to a specific place. There are also those, like Richard Hugo, Hayden Carruth, and Donald Hall, who have identified their spiritual homes with particular regions. But for many other poets of that troubled generation—Ginsberg, Merwin, Rich—the sense of alienation springs from disenchantment with American vulgarity and materialism, rather than from their separation from a particular region. And among poets of my own generation, such as Larry Levis, Stephen Dunn, and Jim Simmerman, the sense of homelessness is even more diffuse. Two recent collections, Simmerman's *Home* (1982) and Dunn's *Local Time* (1986), explore the theme of homelessness and dislocation, but specific localities are scarcely mentioned. For these poets, "home" is not a place on a map but an inward location, a place in the mind.

Not so for the Irish poet, whose *omphalos* is almost always local. Concentration on place endows a poem with a peculiar power. It sharpens the feelings of estrangement. At the same time, it also opens the poet to the charge of parochialism—a charge to which Heaney has been particularly sensitive. In "Belfast" he describes the stages by which he evolved from a "craven provincial" to a "genuine parochial." The source of that distinction is Patrick Kavanagh:

> Parochialism and provincialism are opposites. The provincial has no mind of his own; he does not trust what his eyes see until he has heard what the metropolis—toward which his eyes are turned—has to say on the subject . . .

The parochial mentality on the other hand is never in any doubt about the social and artistic validity of his parish. All great civilizations are based on parochialism. . . .

(*Collected Pruse* [sic], p. 278)

To skeptics that may sound like special pleading, as might Kavanagh's assertion that "parochialism is universal; it deals with fundamentals." Yet Kavanagh's own poems amply support his claim. Even more than Heaney's, they rise from the experience of a particular parish, fondly remembered.

The parish is that of Inniskeen, in County Monaghan, where Kavanagh lived and farmed for his first thirty-five years. Kavanagh complained that the "stony grey soil" of Monaghan "burgled [his] bank of youth," and his best-known poem, *The Great Hunger* (1942), chronicles the sexual and spiritual deprivations of a peasant farmer. But even after he had moved to Dublin, where he became a combative journalist and a literary celebrity, Kavanagh fashioned his best poems from his memories of Monaghan. He remained a "half-faithed ploughman," "in exile with an unsteady heart."

Kavanagh's Monaghan is an impoverished midland county. Its landscape is not dramatic or picturesque, but it has its own uncanny beauty. Under grey skies and shining mists, its ploughed fields take on an eerie light, and its low drumlins look dark but approachable—hills on a human scale. Yellow gorse—or whin, as it is called there—hedges the tiny tillage fields, inscribing yellow lines against the prevailing green. Along the horizon, where the fields divide, the silhouettes of whin bushes create the shapes that stirred Kavanagh's youthful imagination, making an indelible mark:

> My child poet picked out the letters
> On the grey stone,
> In silver the wonder of a Christmas townland,
> The winking glitter of a frosty dawn.
> ⊰⊱

The Pressed Melodeon

Cassiopeia was over
Cassidy's hanging hill,
I looked and three whin bushes rode across
The horizon—the Three Wise Kings.

An old man passing said:
'Can't he make it talk'—
The melodeon. I hid in the doorway
And tightened the belt of my box-pleated coat.

("A Christmas Childhood")

Thus Kavanagh spiritualizes his native landscape, recording his mystical intuitions. "I wasn't really a writer," he maintains in his autobiography. "I had seen a strange beautiful light on the hills and that was all."[4]

Kavanagh died in 1967. He is buried in Inniskeen, where he is also vividly remembered. At the village crossroads, near the churchyard, a handwritten copy of one of his poems has been reproduced in holograph. And should the curious visitor venture a question or two, he will be regaled with stories—more than can be credited or digested. There is the story of Kavanagh not changing his underwear for a year, or of local girls throwing stones at his bicycle as he pedaled by. More reliably, there are stories of Kavanagh as dreamer and desultory farmer.

"I knew Paddy," a local farmer told me, as he gathered potatoes in a freshly ploughed field. "His mother couldn't read or write, you know. His father was a shoemaker. Paddy's fields were over there—over there. He was not a good farmer surely. Not good at all. He read his books in the fields—kept them in the fences there, between the stones. That's all the heed he paid to his fields. His brother Peter is a smart boy. He lives in New York now . . ."

Kavanagh did, in fact, pay heed to his fields, though his atten-

---

[4]Patrick Kavanagh, *The Green Fool* (New York: Penguin Books, Inc., 1971), p. 239.

tion was that of an elegist. In "Shancoduff," published in 1937, two years before Kavanagh left County Monaghan, he broods on his neglected farmlands:

> My black hills have never seen the sun rising,
> Eternally they look north towards Armagh.
> Lot's wife would not be salt if she had been
> Incurious as my black hills that are happy
> When dawn whitens Glassdrummond chapel.
>
> My hills hoard the bright shillings of March
> While the sun searches in every pocket.
> They are my Alps and I have climbed the Matterhorn
> With a sheaf of hay for three perishing calves
> In the field under the Big Forth of Rocksavage.
>
> The sleety winds fondle the rushy beards of Shancoduff
> While the cattle-drovers sheltering in the Featherna Bush
> Look up and say: 'Who owns them hungry hills
> That the water-hen and snipe must have forsaken?
> A poet? Then by heavens he must be poor.'
> I hear and is my heart not badly shaken?

At once a paean and a valediction, Kavanagh's poem creates a moral landscape. Like Lot's wife, his hills face away from Sodom's evils and north towards Armagh, seat of spiritual authority. This moral geography reinforces the central tension in the poem—the conflict of spiritual and worldly values. On the one hand, there is the white chapel, the farmer's errand of mercy, the silver light. On the other, there are the cattle-drovers, who pass a mercenary judgment on the poet and his land.

Kavanagh's moralized landscape may remind American readers of Frost's, but the differences are, I think, more instructive than the similarities. In either case the poet stands somewhat to the side of his community, endorsing regional pieties but removing himself, by dint of his vocation, from the work of ordinary people. Yet Kavanagh's idiom, unlike Frost's, rises unselfconsciously from the spoken language of his parish, its awkwardness intact, its grammar uncorrected. It is a countryman's speech, but it does not seem grafted, as Frost's often does, nor is it splayed over the framework of blank verse. Though an outsider, the poet is at one with the speech of his community, even as he bids Shancoduff farewell.

Kavanagh's move to Dublin was probably inevitable. His instincts drove him to the center of literary culture. Yet by uprooting himself he ruptured the unity of self and environment, speech and place, which is one of his greatest strengths. Though he could still write touching poems from his memories of Monaghan, his work of the forties is an embarrassment—a medley of ugly doggerel, self-indulgent satire, and journalistic sniping, most of it parochial in a way we cannot admire. In 1955, while recuperating from major surgery, he found a second home on the banks of the Grand Canal, near the Baggot Street Bridge, where he experienced a spiritual rebirth. There, in a spirit of self-surrender, he wrote a celebrated group of sonnets, which recover the simplicity—if not the earthiness—of his early verse:

> Leafy-with-love banks and the green waters of the canal
> Pouring redemption for me, that I do
> The will of God, wallow in the habitual, the banal,
> Grow with nature again as before I grew.
> The bright stick trapped, the breeze adding a third
> Party to the couple kissing on an old seat,
> And a bird gathering materials for the nest for the Word
> Eloquently new and abandoned to its delirious beat.
> O unworn world enrapture me, encapture me in a web
> Of fabulous grass and eternal voices by a beech,
> Feed the gaping need of my senses, give me ad lib
> To pray unselfconsciously with overflowing speech
> For this soul needs to be honoured with a new dress woven
> From green and blue things and arguments that cannot be proven.[5]

---

[5]Patrick Kavanagh, "Canal Bank Walk," in *Complete Poems* (New York: Peter Kavanagh Hand Press, 1984), pp. 294–295.

If these lines evoke a saintly equanimity, the stories one hears in Dublin suggest quite the opposite. Or rather, they color an already complex impression of a man whom everyone claims to have known, or loved, or intensely disliked. What is most often recalled is Kavanagh's abusive criticism, his insults to fellow writers, his battles with alcohol and physical decline. All were aggravated by his sense of uprootedness, which shortened his life and put a curse on his work. Yet he has cast a long shadow on contemporary Irish poetry, and no new poet can afford to ignore his example.

Kavanagh lived in Dublin in the forties and fifties—a period of wartime neutrality, censorship, and literary doldrums. In retrospect his world seems less than alluring, but it also seems a good deal simpler and more coherent than the world of his successors. Kavanagh detested the notion of "Irishness" in writing, and rejected the idea of Ireland as a spiritual entity. But from the vantage point of the eighties, one is struck by Kavanagh's freedom even to consider such an idea—a luxury lost to contemporary Irish poets.

Dervla Murphy (in *Ireland*, Salem House, 1985) has compared present-day Ireland to a jigsaw puzzle, whose pieces have yet to be joined, or even found. Murphy's perception, as it relates to personal identity, is borne out by the work of Aidan Carl Mathews, Thomas McCarthy, and other poets of the Republic, and it is even more evident in the work of Derek Mahon, John Hewitt, Paul Muldoon, and other poets of Northern Ireland, who, as Seamus Heaney reminds us, must continually ask the question, "What is my nation?" In his novel *Nothing Happens in Carmincross* (Boston: Godine, 1985), Benedict Kiely captures the confusion exactly:

Two faces of our Ulster, Mervyn, hapless, hopeless province or country or six counties, or nine counties, or U.K., or unrecovered Ireland, or whatever in hell or out of it you like to call it. (p. 189)

The six counties are those of Northern Ireland. The nine are those of historic Ulster. Three of those counties—Monaghan,

Cavan, and Donegal—became part of the Republic after 1922, but in the minds of many, they remain part of their historic province, whatever the political divisions. Thus even the boundaries of one's nation, let alone one's national identity, are open to question.

The poets of the North have responded to their dilemma in varying ways. Seamus Heaney has called up the spirits of his Derry childhood. More recently he has probed his Catholic roots and insisted publicly on his Irish identity. John Hewitt (b. 1907) has limned the Protestant mind of Ulster for half a century, while delineating his distance from country people. In sharp contrast, Derek Mahon has turned his attention outward, casting his lot with other writers in exile. Some of Mahon's most memorable poems are verse letters to friends living in London and Greece, meditations on European paintings, and imitations of Corbière, Cavafy, Nerval, and other European writers. Though steeped in Irish history, he has taken Europe rather than Ulster as his province. And he has taken, as his mentors, not Yeats or Kavanagh but Auden and MacNeice, whose poems are touchstones for his own urbane, epigrammatic meditations.

Mahon was born in 1941 and grew up in Belfast. After a university education at Trinity College, Dublin, he lived in France and North America before settling in London in 1970. Although he has distanced himself, geographically and psychologically, from both the Troubles and the beauty of his native province, he has returned often in his poems, bearing a cargo of guilt, bitterness, and unrequited longings. In "Ecclesiastes," he casts a satiric eye on the dour zealotry of Ulster Calvinists, who can "wear black, drink water, nourish a fierce zeal / with locusts and wild honey, and not / feel called upon to understand and forgive / but only to speak with a bleak / afflatus . . ." In "'Songs of Praise,'" he looks askance at local parishioners, who "lift up their hymnbooks and their hearts / To please the outside-broadcast cameras." Yet elsewhere he praises the landscape of Donegal, where the hills are "a deeper green / Than anywhere in the world," and he dreams of Inishere while living in Cambridge, Massachusetts. In "Afterlives," a poem expressing deep misgivings, he returns to Belfast, pondering the life he might have led:

> And I step ashore in a fine rain
> To a city so changed
> By five years of war
> I scarcely recognize
> The places I grew up in,
> The faces that try to explain.
>
> But the hills are still the same
> Grey-blue above Belfast.
> Perhaps if I'd stayed behind
> And lived it bomb by bomb
> I might have grown up at last
> And learnt what is meant by home.[6]

Yet even this ambivalent *mea culpa* engages Mahon's prevailing irony. "Home," one notes, is made to rhyme with "bomb."

In "The Sea in Winter," a verse letter written from Portrush, County Antrim, to a fellow poet living in Greece, Mahon again takes up the theme of personal identity. The polarities of north and south create a central tension in Mahon, as in Thomas Mann:

> When I returned one year ago
> I felt like Tonio Kröger—slow
> To come to terms with my own past
> Yet knowing I could never cast
> Aside the things that made me what,
> For better or worse, I am. The upshot?
> Chaos and instability,
> The cool gaze of the RUC.

---

[6]Derek Mahon, *Poems 1962–1978* (New York: Oxford University Press, 1979).

Here the instability of the province creates its reflection in the mind of its poet, and the cool gaze of the Royal Ulster Constabulary has its counterpart in Mahon's sober self-appraisal.

"Beyond Howth Head," another verse letter, presents an unsparing view of modern Ireland and envisions one means of escape:

> Spring lights the country. From a thousand
> Dusty corners, house by house,
> From under beds and vacuum cleaners,
> Empty Kosangas containers,
> Bread bins, car seats, crates of stout,
> The first flies cry to be let out,
> To cruise a kitchen, find a door
> And die clean in the open air
>
> Whose smokeless clarity distills
> A chisel's echo in the hills
> As if some Noah, weather-wise,
> Could read a deluge in clear skies.
> But nothing ruffles the wind's breath:
> This peace is the sweet peace of death
> Or *l'outre-tombe*. Make no noise,
> The foxes have quit Clonmacnoise.
>
> I too, uncycled, might exchange,
> Since 'we are changed by what we change,'
> My forkful of the general mess
> For hazel-nuts and water-cress
> Like one of those old hermits who,
> Less virtuous than some, withdrew
> From the world-circles women make
> To a small island in a lake.

But would sackcloth suit so suave a persona? More to the point, would the hermit's ahistorical locale, his private Innisfallen, suffice for a poet haunted by the past? These lines echo Eliot's *Preludes* ("From a thousand / Dusty corners . . .") and quote from Auden's *New Year Letter* ("We are changed by what we change"). Their meter and manner also recall Auden's epistolary verse, and they allude to a ninth-century Irish poem which describes foxes eating human corpses after the Danes sacked Clonmacnoise. Should he seriously want to step outside history, literary or political, this poet will have much to forget.

Mahon's dilemma resembles that of Stephen Dedalus, who would fly by the nets of history. It also has parallels in the work of Mahon's contemporaries, who struggle both to remember and to forget their country's past, to grapple with history and to live outside it altogether. Such tensions impel John Montague to return to County Tyrone, even as he longs to have done with the "dolmens round [his] childhood." They compel Thomas Kinsella, in "A Country Walk," to turn away from the present moment and into the boneyards of Irish history. And they lead Seamus Heaney, in *North*, to rummage Jutland's bogs for "symbols adequate to our predicament." In the sacrificial victims preserved in Danish bogs, Heaney finds emblems for the sectarian violence in Northern Ireland. It is a way of distancing that violence—and of settling the quarrel of artist and witness, which has vexed Heaney throughout his career.

Not everyone has been satisfied with Heaney's solution, or with his formulation of the problem. To find symbols for a predicament sounds to Kinsella like "finding an image to allay my toothache." Similarly, Paul Muldoon has argued that "we are involved in a process not a predicament"—a process which an Irish poet ignores at his peril. Heaney acknowledges as much in "Exposure," where he speaks from a temporary retreat in County Wicklow. By leaving Northern Ireland he has "escaped from the massacre," but perhaps he has also "missed / The once-in-a-life-time portent, / The comet's pulsing rose."

In more recent poems, such as "Sandstone Keepsake," Heaney

explores the pressure of political events on a neutral, contemplative poet:

> It is a kind of chalky russet
> solidified gourd, sedimentary
> and so reliably dense and bricky
> I often clasp it and throw it from hand to hand.
>
> It was ruddier, with an underwater
> hint of contusion, when I lifted it,
> wading a shingle beach on Inishowen.
> Across the estuary light after light
>
> came on silent round the perimeter
> of the camp. A stone from Phlegethon,
> bloodied on the bed of hell's hot river?
> Evening frost and the salt water
>
> made my hand smoke, as if I'd plucked the heart
> that damned Guy de Montfort to the boiling flood—
> but not really, though I remembered
> his victim's heart in its casket, long venerated.
>
> Anyhow, there I was with the wet red stone
> in my hand, staring across at the watch-towers
> from my free state of image and allusion,
> swooped on, then dropped by trained binoculars:
>
> a silhouette not worth bothering about,
> out for the evening in scarf and waders
> and not about to set times wrong or right,
> stooping along, one of the venerators.[7]

This self-deprecating meditation places Heaney's persona in County Donegal, at the border between the Republic and North-

---

[7]Seamus Heaney, *Station Island* (Winchester, Md.: Faber & Faber, Inc., 1984), p. 20.

ern Ireland. It also aligns him with history's witnesses, whose lives about the sites of violent events. What begins as a sentimental reminiscence becomes a vision of infernal violence, wherein the estuary of Lough Foyle becomes the mythical river of fire, and Northern Ireland becomes a contemporary Hades.

In Heaney's imagination, the keepsake becomes the heart of Prince Henry of Cornwall, murdered by de Montfort in the Church of San Silvestro, Viterbo, in 1271. It is the heart which, according to Dante (*Inferno*, XII 118–20), still drips blood upon the Thames, having been placed atop a pillar at the end of London Bridge. Analogously, here on his northern waterway, Heaney becomes one of the pious spectators—the venerators—who gaze with awe on the evidence of violent deeds. He in turn is watched, until his British observers dismiss him as unthreatening.

Despite its informal tone, Heaney's self-portrait is deeply self-critical. It is, in its way, an act of penance. But what, in fact, are his alternatives? What else is he to do? Heaney's "free state" is that of the artist, whose freedom must not be compromised by ideology. The phrase itself puns on the Republic's original name, while affirming the poet's right of detachment. Buried in Heaney's allusion to Dante is a further byplay—a reference to the disputed lines "Colui fesse in grembo a Dio / lo cor che 'n su Tamisi ancor si cola." In one interpretation, *cola* derives from *colere* (to venerate); in another, it derives from *colare* (to flow, to drip). Here Heaney manages to have it both ways: the heart drips and is venerated. And Heaney becomes one of the venerators, while holding the dripping heart.

Is such cleverness self-indulgence, when contrasted with the realities of gelignite and plastic bullets? Or, to put the question another way, "Is Ireland sober really and truly Ireland free?"

The last question is Benedict Kiely's, and although I have taken it out of context, it bears directly on the situation of the Irish poet. Eight hundred years of conflict underlie the latest mortar attack in Newry, the latest bomb in South Armagh. Is a sober, elegiac attitude the only appropriate response to such events, or to the process of which they are a part? What limits does this unignorable subject place on the freedom of the Irish poet, who might prefer to be more playful, or to attend to ahistorical themes?

It is self-evident that Heaney and his contemporaries are not free to ignore the sorrows of their homeland, or to poeticize other people's griefs. Such freedom as they have stems rather from the poet's traditional prerogatives—the right to elect a tone, to shape experience, to adjust the distance between speaker and event, audience and persona. There is also the possibility, however elusive, that sectarian conflicts will be transcended, either through tragic awareness or through comic detachment.

The tragic theme has come naturally to Irish poets, from Yeats to Mangan to Eibhlín Dhubh Ni Chonaill. It is, perhaps, the indigenous tone in a nation which, as Kavanagh observes, never forgets the fact of death, even when building a house. In *The Green Fool*, Kavanagh tells this revealing story:

> When the new house was finished Peter Hamill, a dear friend of father's, came to see it. I heard him say to father: "Ye'll have to be taken out the window if ye die upstairs."
>
> Father said he didn't care how his coffin was taken out. The landing top of the stairs was too short on which to turn a coffin.
>
> People in Ireland never forget that they have to die. Even at the building of a new house the thought of the last going out was in somebody's mind.

Among the Irish peasantry Yeats detected a "perpetual Last Day, a trumpeting and coming to judgement." In the twilights of Ireland, as in the temper of the Aran Islanders, Synge found a "vague but passionate anguish."

Among contemporary Irish writers, the poet who has sounded the tragic note most persistently is Thomas Kinsella, a committed nationalist and a profound interpreter of Irish history. Kinsella recently described himself as a "poet of memories and dreams," and of late his work has turned increasingly inward. In his early poems, however, he often looks outward, exploring a sense of loss that transcends the merely personal. In one haunting elegy, he places the Irish Renaissance in the stream of history:

MAGNANIMITY
(for Austin Clarke's seventieth birthday)

> '*So I forgot*
> *His enmity.*'

Green abundance

Last summer in Coole Park. A stone hearth
Surviving; a grassy path by the orchard wall.

You stared through chicken-wire at the initials
Cut in Lady Gregory's tree, scars grown thick.
Overhead a breath passed magniloquently through the leaves,

Branches swayed and sank. You turned away and said
Coole might be built again as a place for poets.
Through the forbidden tree magnanimity passed.

I am sure that there are no places for poets,
Only changing habitations for verse to outlast.
Your own house, isolated by a stream, exists

For your use while you live—like your body and your world.
Helpless commonness encroaches, chews the soil,
Squats ignobly. Within, consciousness intensifies:

Sharp small evils magnify into Evil,
Pity and mockery suggest some idea of Good,
Fright stands up stiffly under pain of death.

Houses shall pass away, and all give place
To signposts and chicken-wire.

A tree stands.

Pale cress persists on a shaded stream.[8]

---

[8]Thomas Kinsella, *Poems 1956–1973* (Winston-Salem: Wake Forest University Press, 1979), p. 95.

The Pressed Melodeon

Austin Clarke was born in 1896, Kinsella in 1928. Written midway in its author's life, this reflection celebrates the longevity of a poet whose career spans the distance between Yeats's generation and Kinsella's own. It is appropriate that the ruins of Coole Park should be likened to the private house and the mortal body of Austin Clarke, a poet closely associated with Yeats, the Celtic Twilight, and the Abbey Theater. Here Clarke becomes a survivor, a reminder of that brief radiance in Irish literary history. The commonplace metaphor—body-as-house, house-as-body—takes on new life in its new environs.

Kinsella's elegy is in part a tribute to Lady Gregory, whose benevolence nurtured the Irish Renaissance. More broadly, it is a nationalist's gesture of gratitude, a conciliatory salute. For Kavanagh the Irish Renaissance was a "thoroughgoing English-bred lie," a fabrication of the Anglo-Irish Ascendancy. But in Kinsella's more generous vision, Coole Park becomes a magnanimous hospice, now sadly gone to ruin. Class rivalry and partisan enmity give away to forgiveness. And Kinsella's lament for an older order, his complaint against encroaching vulgarity, gives way to a spirit of acceptance—a magnanimity in the poet as well as his subject. The process of aging is accepted, as is the passing away of noble houses. The poem ends in affirmation, with a hint of tragic exultation.

Austin Clarke celebrated his seventieth birthday in 1966, three years before the eruption of violence in Belfast and Derry. In the presence of daily tragedy, has any poet maintained Kinsella's calm, philosophical detachment? And further, has any poet rediscovered the sources of redemptive laughter, the repose and detachment that Kavanagh thought essential to great poetry? For tragedy, Kavanagh said, is "undeveloped comedy." The "mark of a poet," he insisted, "is his lightness, the pure personality revealed bare in all its volatility and with the gaiety that is of God."[9]

Among contemporary Irish poets one must look far to find the lightness Kavanagh sought. Nor is gaiety to be expected in a country with Ireland's repressive laws, the highest unemployment rate in Europe, increasing crime in Dublin, and the interminable conflict in the North. Yet gaiety of a kind can be found, most notably in the poems of Paul Muldoon, who has lived in Belfast for the past nine years. Muldoon's comedy is more often sardonic than redemptive, but it captures the grim absurdities and bizarre incongruities of a seventeen-year-old struggle, as (in "Aisling") it plays irreverently with traditional Irish themes:

> I was making my way home late one night
> this summer, when I staggered
> into a snow drift.
>
> Her eyes spoke of a sloe-year,
> her mouth a year of haws.
>
> Was she Aurora, or the goddess Flora,
> Artemidora, or Venus bright,
> or Anorexia, who left
> a lemon stain on my flannel sheet?
>
> It's all much of a muchness.
>
> In Belfast's Royal Victoria Hospital
> a kidney machine
> supports the latest hunger-striker
> to have called off his fast, a saline
> drip into his bag of brine.
>
> A lick and a promise. Cuckoo spittle.
> I hand my sample to Doctor Maw.
> She gives me back a confident *All Clear*.[10]

An *aisling* (pronounced *ash-ling*) is a vision of a young woman symbolizing Irish freedom. A traditional motif in Irish poetry, it

[9]Patrick Kavanagh, *November Haggard: Uncollected Prose and Verse*, ed. Peter Kavanagh (New York: The Peter Kavanagh Head Press, 1971), p. 57.

[10]Paul Muldoon, *Quoof* (Winchester, Md.: Faber & Faber, Inc., 1983), p. 39.

becomes for Muldoon a twisted surrealistic vision, a bewildering spectacle, juxtaposed with the latest evidence of futile Irish rebellion. "It's all much of a muchness" strikes the note of detachment—or resignation. That may not be the comic detachment Kavanagh had in mind, but it is probably all that is possible in Irish poetry just now.

THE LIGHTNESS Kavanagh spoke of may, in fact, be found more often in Ireland's prose writers, particularly Flann O'Brien and Benedict Kiely, than in postwar Irish poets. Whether one will influence the other remains to be seen, but certainly Kiely has Kavanagh's lightness of touch, and in *Nothing Happens in Carmincross* he makes a black, bitter comedy of the situation in the North.

In one episode of that novel, a native of Tyrone, pottering in his garden, is startled by the sudden appearance of a black British soldier on his property. The soldier, equally startled, asks: "Man, what you doing here?"—to which the Tyrone man gives this reply:

> So I says to him, man o'dear, whoever you are and wherever you come from and however you got the rigout, but that's a curious question. The Timoneys, you may never have heard of them, but I'm one of them and we're here since a bit before the time that Hugh O'Neill of Dungannon had the spot of trouble with Queen Elizabeth of England, not the present nice wee cutty that I saw once in Derry city on a visit, no the other Elizabeth long ago that cut the head of many's the man, and Timoneys were here then and have been here since, and we know where we came from before that, and what I would ask you, man o'dear, is another question and that is what in the name of the merciful Jasus are you doing here?
>
> —A pungent question, Mervyn said.

(p. 201)

There, in small, is the Irish predicament—and one cathartic response. In this bizarre anecdote, Kiely has captured the sense of roots and the pain of dispossession, the invader's foolish arrogance, the disagreement that so easily turns lethal. And, in antic prose that seems scarcely to touch the page, he has offered a curative vision, a way of coping with a tragic situation.

As of this writing, the situation in the North appears to be getting worse. Ulster Unionists have taken to the streets to protest the new Anglo-Irish agreement, which gives Dublin a modest voice in the affairs of Northern Ireland. That agreement also brings the country one step closer to reunification—a prospect that frightens Unionists, who are loyal to the Queen. The Apprentice Boys of Derry, a Unionist organization, have announced their plans to march, and a new round of violence is expected.

Despite these unhappy developments, I plan to visit Ireland again in the near future, in the hope of learning a bit more about the Irish poet's situation, past and present. "Many countries today," writes Benedict Kiely, "have much worse and, therefore, more interesting situations than Ireland" (*Nothing Happens in Carmincross*, p. 220). That acerbic comment should humble any American visitor who finds the Irish predicament *merely* interesting, or is of a mind to make pronouncements on other people's sorrows. At the same time, I believe an American writer has much to learn by studying recent Irish poetry—and a few things to envy in the Irish poet's situation.

In the first place, it is heartening to visit an English-speaking country where the idea of the poet is still taken seriously. Irish writers complain that their culture pays lip service to Poetry while neglecting poets and letting national treasures like Coole Park fall into ruin. Their point is well taken, but it is pleasing, nonetheless, to visit a country where poems are reproduced in holograph on village monuments, where the faces of poets—Swift, Yeats— appear on paper currency, where full-time writers are exempt from income tax, and where poets like Kavanagh are remembered so passionately, both by poets and by lay people.

In the second place, it is instructive to encounter, first hand, the

Irish historical outlook as it bears on the definition of personal identity. Asked to define themselves, American poets are likely to rummage memories from childhood, recall dreams, or invoke archetypal imagery. An Irish poet, asked the same question, is likely to investigate parish history, or examine genealogies, or piece together an identity from fragments of local lore. Provincial —or parochial—as that may sound, it is a way of thinking that has very nearly been lost in American poetry, and it is well worth encountering again. And, as Donald Hall reminds us, "provinciality is compatible with great literature in a country with a long history."

Finally, it is revealing to visit a country where one's own language matters so much, and where English words carry so much power, political and otherwise. Everyone has heard of the Irish gift of the gab, the love of talk and storytelling. What is less often recognized is the power of language in a country so politicized, so keenly aware of nuances and innuendoes. To speak of "Northern Ireland" rather than "the North" is to give legitimacy to a hated division. To speak of the "Catholic Church" rather than "the Church" is to betray a pluralistic outlook. To order a "half" of Guinness rather than a "glass" is to express allegiance with Ulster. And so on, and so on.

Certain words also have power to silence a room, even when spoken softly. I recall the evening in a crowded Monaghan pub, six miles from the border, when a friend, describing his travels in the Middle East, uttered the word *checkpoint*. The room fell silent— though a moment before, there had been a low din and no sign of anyone listening. As my friend went on to explain, as coolly and audibly as he could, that he was speaking of Israel, the tension eased, and the din gradually returned. But as I reflect on it now, I cannot recall when a single, innocent word, spoken among strangers, has carried more resonance or power.

1986

Selective Laurels[1]

To the etymologist an anthology is a gathering of flowers, but to poets, critics, and other interested parties it is almost always a political statement. It swears allegiances and announces disavowals. It redresses grievances—and often creates new ones. If the poems happen to be Irish, the statement will be uncommonly charged, for Irish poetry is today a welter of conflicting allegiances and loyalties, conventions and traditions. Beneath the obvious topographical, political, and religious divisions—North and South, British and Gaelic, rural and urban, Protestant and Catholic—lies a more profound rift between two languages and their attendant traditions. On the one side there is the Anglo-Irish tradition, whose language is Hiberno-English and whose bloodline runs from Swift, Goldsmith, and Sheridan to Mangan, Ferguson, Davis, and Yeats. On the other there is a native tradition, whose language is Irish-Gaelic and whose treasures include early monastic poems, charms, prayers, courtly verse, *Buile Suibhne*, "The Hag of Beare," and four centuries of bardic poetry. Any new poem by Seamus Heaney or Thomas Kinsella will steer an uneasy course between those rivaling traditions. And any new anthology is bound to reveal a bias, however balanced it may appear.

---

[1]Thomas Kinsella, editor, *The New Oxford Book of Irish Verse*, Oxford University Press, 1986. Paul Muldoon, editor, *The Faber Book of Contemporary Irish Poetry*. Faber and Faber, 1986.

Thomas Kinsella has long since taken sides, both as the author of an anti-British broadside and as the leading translator of poetry from the Irish. In "Butcher's Dozen" (1972) Kinsella recalled the violence of Bloody Sunday and alleged a coverup by the Widgery Tribunal. In his editorial role he has more subtly attacked those literary prejudices which venerate the Anglo-Irish canon and demote the native tradition. Kinsella's translation of *The Tain* (1969) made the eighth-century saga available to the general reader and reasserted its importance in world literature. His translations of three centuries of Irish verse, collected in *An Duanaire*, have done much to make Irish poets—and American readers—aware of an endangered heritage. And now, in his radical revision of *The Oxford Book of Irish Verse* (1958) he has taken his effort one step further, setting his new translations of Irish poetry beside the Anglo-Irish canon. His stated purpose is to "present an idea of these two bodies of poetry and of the relationships between them." His achievement is to chronicle the flowering and decline of the oldest vernacular poetry in Western Europe.

Kinsella's selections tell a melancholy story. Beginning with a poem in praise of St. Colum Cille (A.D. 597) and ending with Michael Hartnett's "A Farewell to English" (1975), Kinsella's history spans fourteen centuries, placing well-known Anglo-Irish poems beside obscure or famous Irish texts. The balance is never even—and never easy. From the sixth through the twelfth centuries a mixture of Christianity and pagan naturalism, Latin and vernacular Irish gives rise to songs, prayers, epitaphs and lyrics of sensuous immediacy, notably those attributed to Colum Cille ("I am sad for the tearful cries / from the two shores of Loch Febail: / the cries of Conall and Eogan / lamenting as I left"). Over the next four centuries a body of candid love poetry emerges, concurrent with the work of the bardic order, whose era begins with eulogies for local chieftains and ends with laments for their own dispossession. After the Cromwellian wars the vitality of Irish poetry quickly dwindles, as the once-privileged bards become outcasts, and such survivors as Aogán Ó Rathaille and Dáibhí Ó Bruadair are left to mourn a fading culture. By the end of the nineteenth century, its vernacular eroded by famine and oppression, poetry in Irish has suffered the fate of the Irish harp, despite the efforts of Mangan and Ferguson to bring it back to life. Little wonder that the tenor of Irish verse, from the Flight of the Earls to the ascendancy of Yeats, largely embraces sounds of lamentation, relieved by Brian Merriman's "The Midnight Court" and other moments of comedy and satire.

Kinsella's anthology is not the first to tell this rueful tale. Its most recent forbear is John Montague's *Faber Book of Irish Verse* (1974), which includes many of the same texts. What distinguishes Kinsella's book is both his scholarly thoroughness and his almost total reliance upon his own translations. Where Montague drew on the work of many hands, Kinsella has left his distinctive mark on nearly every poem.

Here, for example, are two versions of a stanza from Piaras Feiritéar (c. 1600-1653):

> Gentlest of women, put your weapons by,
> Unless you want to ruin all mankind;
> Leave the assault or I must make reply,
> Proclaiming that you are murderously inclined.
> Put by your armour, lay your darts to rest,
> Hide your soft hair and all its devious ways;
> To see it lie in coils upon your breast
> Poisons all hope and mercilessly slays.
>
> —Trans. Eiléan Ni Chuilleanáin

> Lay your weapons down, young lady.
>   Do you want to ruin us all?
> Lay your weapons down, or else
>   I'll have you under royal restraint.

-◂-

These weapons put behind you:
hide henceforth your curling hair;
do not bare that white breast
that spares no living man.

—Trans. Thomas Kinsella

Here Kinsella's drift is toward greater physicality and away from the clichés of English verse. The conventional tropes of slaying, darts, and armor give way to the stark image of a bare white breast.

Elsewhere Kinsella restores Irish proper names and place-names, recovering the strangeness of the originals:

O if he lived, the prince who sheltered me
And his company who gave me entry
On the river of the Laune,
Whose royalty stood sentry
Over intricate harbors, I and my own
Would not be desolate in Dermot's country.

—Aogán Ó Rathaille, "A Time of Change"
—Trans. Eavan Boland

If that guardian King from the bank of the Leamhan lived on,
with all who shared his fate (and would pity my plight)
to rule that soft, snug region, bayed and harboured,
my people would not stay poor in Duibhne country.

—Trans. Thomas Kinsella

Here Kinsella's rendering bespeaks an intimacy with landscape, while honoring the tradition of the *Dinnshenchas*—the lore and legendry of place-names. It also sends us to his extensive notes, where we learn that Duibhne (pronounced *dív-na*) lies on the Dingle Peninsula.

Those of us without Irish cannot judge the fidelity of Kinsella's translations, though their gains in directness seem unassailable. At the same time we can wonder a little at his choices from the

Anglo-Irish tradition, where his taste is at once conventional and idiosyncratic. Old favorites by Goldsmith, Mangan, Davis, and Ferguson are included. Thomas Moore is given a fair hearing. But in the selections from modern Irish verse one is left with the impression that poems have been chosen as much—or more—for their bearing on Irish affairs as for their intrinsic merits. And certain omissions are puzzling.

Kinsella has, for example, included Yeats's "Easter 1916," "To Ireland in the Coming Times," and "Red Hanrahan's Song about Ireland," but not the Byzantium poems or "Leda and the Swan" or "Among School Children." Louis MacNeice's "Autumn Journal" is excluded, as are Patrick Kavanagh's early Monaghan poems and the entirety of *The Great Hunger*. John Montague, author of several book-length sequences, is limited to four minor lyrics; and the choices from Heaney include nothing from *Station Island*—perhaps his most important collection. No doubt considerations of space dictated some of these omissions, but they create imbalances nonetheless, as does the complete absence of women writers after 1800.

Given its breadth and historical depth, Kinsella's anthology should remain an invaluable resource for many years to come. To appreciate the high achievement of modern Irish verse, however, we might do better to look to Paul Muldoon's new anthology, one of the most valuable in the Faber series. Like Kinsella's it is anything but neutral, but it is astutely edited, and it presents some of the best work produced in (or about) Ireland during the past four decades.

Paul Muldoon (b. 1951) is the leading younger poet of Northern Ireland, and it should surprise no one that most of the poets he has chosen come from the North or speak from northern experience. What does give pause is that Muldoon has limited himself, in a book of some four hundred pages, to only ten poets. From the older generation he has included Kavanagh and MacNeice. From the middle generation he has selected Heaney,

Montague, Kinsella, and Michael Longley. And from his own generation he has chosen Tom Paulin, Paul Durcan, Derek Mahon, and Medbh McGuckian. Among the missing are the younger poets of the Republic (Aidan Mathews, Sebastian Barry, Dermot Bolger, Eiléan Ni Chuilleanáin, and others); Denis Devlin, Austin Clarke, and Pearse Hutchinson; Nuala Ní Dhomhnaill and Michael Hartnett (who write in Irish); and Muldoon himself. For some readers these omissions have been grievous, and in Ireland the anthology has come in for harsh criticism. Reviewing the book in the *Irish Times* (June 7, 1986), Derek Mahon feared it would mislead outsiders and hoped it would "sink without a trace."

Mahon's objection is understandable, but from an outsider's standpoint it seems extreme, for if Muldoon's anthology fails to provide an overview of contemporary Irish poetry, it does present verse of a consistently high quality, and its generous allotments allow the identities of ten poets to emerge in bold relief. To lavish attention on Kavanagh and MacNeice, in an anthology of "contemporary" verse, is questionable but defensible, because both poets have shaped postwar Irish verse profoundly and continue to do so.

MacNeice and Kavanagh have often been regarded as near opposites and viewed as the father figures, respectively, of the younger poets of the North and South. Kavanagh was the Catholic mystic with the "clay-heavy mind," the elegist of rural deprivation, who had the "enthusiasm of a man who sees life simply" ("Art McCooey"). By contrast MacNeice was the urban sophisticate who felt "banned forever from the candles of the Irish poor" ("Carrickfergus"). Yet to read ample selections from both poets, side by side, is to see how much they had in common, not only in their hardheaded northern realism but also in their felt sense of exile and their deeply ambivalent attitude toward their native land. In "Temptation in Harvest" Kavanagh opts for Dublin, art, and literature while looking back fondly at his rural Monaghan community, which elsewhere he describes as "hell." Similarly, in

"Valediction," MacNeice denounces Irish feuding and self-delusion while recalling how "quick / Winging shadows of white clouds pass / Over the long hills like a fiddle's phrase." Out of this common quarrel came two widely divergent voices.

The shades of MacNeice and Kavanagh haunt the work of the middle generation, particularly Montague and Heaney. What sets these apart, however, is their receptivity to mid-century American influences and their felt obligation to deal with political turmoil. Kavanagh scoffed at the American muse, and MacNeice took his bearings mainly from England and Europe. By contrast, Heaney has learned as much from Frost and Elizabeth Bishop as he has from Kavanagh, and such poems as "Sloe Gin," "The Otter," and "The Skunk" show the influence of Lowell. Kinsella's abandonment of formal stanzas in midcareer has parallels in the work of American poets, and such poems as Kinsella's "Baggot Street Deserta" and Montague's "A Drink of Milk" are indebted to William Carlos Williams.

Whatever their interest in America, however, poets of Heaney's generation have had, since 1969, a uniquely Irish dilemma to confront. Heaney's response to the Troubles has been to probe Danish bogs and his own guilt-stricken imagination for "images and symbols adequate to our predicament." Kinsella and Longley have, for the most part, turned away from social realism to plumb the wells of memory and dream, while Montague has taken an historical approach, juxtaposing images of contemporary violence with the atrocities of seventeenth-century Ulster. Memorable work has emerged from these responses, most notably Heaney's "The Tollund Man," Longley's "Letter to Derek Mahon," Kinsella's "His Father's Hands," and Montague's "Last Journey."

Muldoon's own generation has yet to produce a comparable achievement. Paul Durcan's satire is witty and jaunty, but soon wears thin. Medbh McGuckian and Tom Paulin, two gifted Belfast poets, offer better verse and a revealing contrast, the first being hermetic and apolitical, the second brittle and outspoken. But for this reader the most impressive is Derek Mahon, whose fastidious control and epigrammatic wit have few contemporary peers, in Ireland or elsewhere. In Mahon's best poems, eloquence joins forces with historical awareness:

> Lost people of Treblinka and Pompeii!
> 'Save us, save us,' they seem to say,
> 'Let the god not abandon us
> Who have come so far in darkness and in pain.
> We too had our lives to live.
> You with your light meter and relaxed itinerary,
> Let not our naive labours have been in vain!'
>
> ("A Disused Shed in Co. Wexford")

It is a tribute to Mahon's integrity that he should rebuke a book that shows him to such advantage. I, for one, hope that both Muldoon's intelligent anthology and Kinsella's more compendious book will find the wide audience they deserve.

1986

In the Shadow of the Gasworks

I

ALTHOUGH HE distrusted literary criticism and regarded the bulk of reviewers as snobs and fools, Louis MacNeice (1907-1963) was both a voluble poet and one of the most prolific literary critics of his time. MacNeice believed that "all literary critics are falsifiers in that they try to disintricate the value or essence of a poem from the poem itself." "[T]he man who reads a poem and likes it," he contended, "is doing something far too subtle for criticism." Yet, for all his distrust, MacNeice took the art of criticism seriously and practiced it regularly, both as reviewer and literary essayist. Lately MacNeice's reputation has been enjoying a revival, and Oxford has recently published Alan Heuser's *Selected Criticism of Louis MacNeice*, revealing what even MacNeice's admirers may have forgotten: that the author of "Bagpipe Music," "Snow," and *Autumn Journal* was also an astringent critic, whose astute perceptions of Yeats, Eliot, Auden, and others still have the power to persuade. Likewise MacNeice's humane example, which was laudable in his time and is even more welcome today.

MacNeice's most important criticism may be found in two books published in his lifetime: *Modern Poetry* (1938), an assessment of Eliot's generation and a defense of his own; and *The Poetry of W.B. Yeats* (1941), a pioneering study. *Varieties of Parable*

(1965), his posthumous book, analyzes "double-level" writing in Beckett, Pinter, and others, while revising his earlier views. In addition to his books, MacNeice published more than three hundred occasional pieces in such periodicals as *The Listener* and *The Spectator*, and otherwise contributed to critical discourse through his prefaces, introductions, film reviews, articles, and radio broadcasts. Combining subtle analysis with a blunt aphoristic style ("The purists are the curse of the arts"; "Mr Pound does not know when to stop; he is a born strummer."), MacNeice addressed the major literary issues of his day, most notably the issue of poetic subject-matter, the debate between Aestheticism and "realism," the proper relationship of poetry to journalism, and the vexed question of poetry and "belief." By temperament a skeptic, MacNeice cast a cool eye on the styles and dogmas of his contemporaries, whether his subject was Eliot's theory of impersonal art, or Auden's "slapdash" methods, or Yeats's balmier beliefs. At his most ardent he could be scathing, as when he excoriates Henry Miller for writing "turgid tatty old-fangled romantic exhibitionist prose, trying so hard to be virile and turning out ham." Little wonder that he found a kindred spirit in Randall Jarrell, another poet-critic who combined the detached appraisal with the bold pronouncement. "There are few contemporary critics," MacNeice lamented, "who show such enthusiasm, honesty, or wit."

MacNeice's quarrel with criticism sprang, in part, from his low opinion of contemporary reviewing. In a public letter to Auden (1937) he defended his friend against the "bevy of second-rate sensitive minds who write in our cultured weeklies." Elsewhere, he satirized the laziness of reviewers who preferred the snap judgment to close analysis:

> According to my reviewers. . . I am a writer they can place quite simply: I am a surprisingly feminine, essentially masculine poet, whose gift is primarily lyrical and basically satirical, swayed by and immune to politics, with and without a religious sense, and I am technically slapdash and technically meticulous, with a

predilection for flat and halting and lilting Swinburnian rhythms, and I have a personal and impersonal approach, with a remarkably wide and consistently narrow range, and I have developed a good deal and I have not developed at all. Most living poets have been similarly treated by reviewers.

Yet MacNeice's objections arose less from indignation than from his awareness of criticism's inherent limitations—and his sense of a vocation betrayed. Criticism, he argued, is by nature inexact. Its judgments are only "approximately true," and it is always on "the verge of self-contradiction." Nevertheless, in the twentieth century the literary critic has assumed a central role. In "Poetry, the Public, and the Critic" (1949) MacNeice portrays the critic as a go-between, who mediates between the difficult modern poem and its often bewildered audience. In an era of specialization and fragmentation, the poet cannot assume that his premises are known to the general public, nor is it his job to state them repeatedly. That is the work of the critic, who will best serve literature by pointing out to the public "what angle a poet is writing from and what he is trying to do." The critic should also serve as analyst of nuance and technical innovation, explicating "such preciser points as the relation between a poet's sentence structure and verse pattern, or his use of the curtain line or his variation of stresses." MacNeice quoted with approval E.M. Forster's definition of the critic's job as "education through precision." Where many critics failed, he thought, was in their lack of genuine critical standards. "And they will not acquire such standards," he insisted, "till they remember that poetry is made with *words*."

And what is the poet's role? From the foregoing, it might be surmised that MacNeice thought of the poet as a remote aesthete, whose musings must be interpreted by the critic for the common reader. In fact, MacNeice's view was quite the opposite. Partly in reaction to Aestheticism and partly in response to the political spirit of the Thirties, MacNeice depicted the poet as an educated common man, gifted and refined but nonetheless "a specialist in something which everyone practices." Throughout *Modern Poetry* he urges a view of the poet as informer, critic, and entertainer, who "uses with precision tools which lie ready to everyone's hand." The poet should be unafraid of vulgarity, frivolity, and sentimentality —attributes he shares with common humanity. He should be "synoptic and elastic in his sympathies," and he should cultivate social awareness, allowing himself to be "penetrated by great events." Toward the end of *Modern Poetry*, MacNeice offers a portrait of the artist as average bloke:

> My own prejudice, then, is in favour of poets whose worlds are not too esoteric. I would have a poet able-bodied, fond of talking, a reader of the newspapers, capable of pity and laughter, informed in economics, appreciative of women, involved in personal relationships, actively interested in politics, susceptible to physical impressions.

In *The Auden Generation* Samuel Hynes suggests that MacNeice's "self-proclaimed role of common man was a kind of substitute for political commitment, a way of being apolitical with a good heart." By contrast, David Perkins (in *A History of Modern Poetry*) sees the idealization of the common man as a reflection of Leftist sympathies and traces it to the influence of Wilfred Owen. Whatever its origin or political stripe, the democratic theme pervades MacNeice's critical thought, overriding his doubts and counter-opinions. At one point MacNeice observes that many poets are "weedy," "short sighted," and " neurotic above the average," but he argues that poetry itself is a normal activity—and a means by which the poet returns to normal. And although he portrays the poetic temperament as a compromise of opposing tendencies—an "unconscious collaboration between Jekyll and Hyde"—he depicts the poet himself as "an ordinary man with specialized gifts," who is at once the spokesman for humanity and its "still, small voice," its conscience and "grievous instinct." All the more reason, then, for criticism to do its work well, healing the unnatural breach between the poet-spokesman and his audience.

Taken in isolation, MacNeice's concept of the poet may seem narrowly traditional—an uneasy fusion of Shelley, Whitman, and Arnold. However, in the evolving dialectics of MacNeice's thought, Arnold contends with I.A. Richards, and the idea of poetry as communication vies with the modernist idea of the poem as autonomous object. In his reflections on the nature, purpose, and subject-matter of poetry, MacNeice often emphasizes the referential and rhetorical elements of his art. "The content of poetry," he declares, "comes out of life." Part critic and part entertainer, the poet is to select subjects which "(a) he is in a position to criticize, and (b) other people are likely to find interesting." At the same time, a poem is a "self-contained entity"; and while it must "correspond (in some way) to life," it must also be "self-coherent," which is to say, it must achieve an equilibrium of opposing elements, a balance of form and content. What makes a good poem, suggests MacNeice, is an even "ratio" between subject and form. "Subject must work itself out in pattern but not be emasculated by pattern."

And how may that ratio be maintained? Or that balance restored? As MacNeice explains it, one reason for writing *Modern Poetry* was to explore the imbalances created by "various conflicting experiments" and to show how modern poetry, particularly that of Auden, Spender, and Day-Lewis, has "set out to readjust the ratio." One of those experiments was the Aesthetic movement of the Nineties, which valued Pure Form at the expense of subject. And in his *apologia* for the Auden group, as represented in Michael Roberts' *New Signatures* anthology (1932), MacNeice is at pains to lift the "dead hand of Pater" and to exorcise the lingering ghosts of Aestheticism. "Art for Art's Sake," he flatly pronounces, "was a doctrine of cowardice"; and though he acknowledges elsewhere that poetry is, to some extent, "autotelic," he has little patience with any doctrine of purity, be it Aestheticism, Symbolism, or Imagism, which values form over subject, feeling over thought, or privileged moments over ordinary life. Taking issue with Wordsworth, he argues that it "is vicious to demand that poetry should always be concerned with 'beauty'. . . or uplift or intense emotion." Intellect can and should play a part equal to that of emotion. For the purpose of poetry is neither the pursuit of beauty nor the recollection of emotion but the providing of entertainment and the conveying of information through the medium of verse. "[S]hould we not again posit," asks MacNeice, "an ideal normal reader, sympathetic to the poet but not a member of his clique, with a natural liking for poetry, of fair education, but without academic bias?" To such an audience the poet will address himself, both as critic and entertainer, and his work will be "only valuable if it can add something to the experience of its public, this addition often consisting merely in the illumination of that public's own experience."

Three years later, in *The Poetry of W.B. Yeats*, MacNeice widened his outlook. In his preface to the later book, he rebukes himself for promulgating a one-sided view of poetry:

> There is not, to my knowledge—nor do I think there can be—any satisfactory definition of the relationship of poetry to life. I am convinced, however, that there is such a relationship and that it is of primary importance; I am also convinced that a poem is a thing in itself, a self-contained organism. . . The literary critic, being unable to assess thinghood, inevitably concerns himself with poetry as correspondence. Such criticism can be valuable but it never rises above what Aristotle called "bastard reasoning". . . Thus in my book, *Modern Poetry*, I overstressed the half-truth that poetry is *about* something, is communication. So it is, but it is also a separate self. . .

Yet MacNeice could not dispose so readily of his bias toward subject-matter, especially topical and political subjects. That bias governs his study of Yeats and his occasional pieces of the Thirties, leading him to praise Auden for writing poems that "can walk in the street without falling flat" and to value public poems like Yeats's "Easter 1916" over poems of the personal life.

MacNeice deplored the prejudice of realists who made subject-matter their chief criterion. But he also deplored the attitude, expressed by certain Imagists and advocates of Pure Form, that subject-matter is unimportant—that any subject will do. "I consider no subject-matter taken from life to be alien to poetry," MacNeice asserted, echoing prevailing opinion. Yet he also demanded that the chosen subject deeply engage the poet's heart and mind:

> I would say that the poet may write about anything, provided that that thing matters to him to start with, for then it will bring with it into the poem the intellectual or emotional or moral significance which it has for him in life. And without such significance a poem has no backbone.

Moreover, certain subjects are likely to produce better—that is, more honest—writing. In his discussion of "Easter 1916" Mac-Neice rejects the opinion that Yeats's poem is more important or more "realistic" because it deals with a contemporary historical event. At the same time, he makes a persuasive case for public over private subjects:

> We can say at the most that many poets—including, I think, Yeats—are more likely to write well, that is with clarity, strength, and emotional honesty, when they are writing about something which has moved them *and others* in their own time than when they are writing about something which belongs more exclusively to their own private mythology . . . And the poet . . . is more likely to shoot truly when he knows that there are many real readers who have knowledge of the matter which he is treating.

Consistent with this view, MacNeice elsewhere chides Eliot for burdening images with private meanings and for using a "private, archaic, and slightly affected mythology."

To give precedence to topical subjects is of course to bring the values of journalism into aesthetic discourse—a danger to which MacNeice was particularly alert. "The facts outside a poem," he reminds us, "the facts which occasion a poem, are no longer the same facts when they have been fused into a poem." And he regards as "vicious" any criticism which assumes that a poem is a "mere translation of facts." At the same time, MacNeice believed, with Auden, that a good writer must be first a good reporter, and that "the normal poet includes the journalist," but must not be "subservient" to him. In the verse and prose of Gerard Manley Hopkins, MacNeice found a quality, "which makes life liveable and writings readable—an inquisitive interest in the objective world, a passion to record it precisely." And he took issue with Arthur Symons and the early Yeats for banishing explicit description from poetry:

> [In his early poems Yeats] was avoiding both description and rhetoric, two characteristics of the journalist. A wider view of poetry might have made him less severe upon journalism. Verlaine was no journalist but what about Villon? Verlaine was no rhetorician but what about Shakespeare or Dante or the Greeks?

In a similar vein, MacNeice defends Auden and Spender. Both permit topical events to enter their poetry, but both remain poets rather than journalists because they "approach their subject, though an outside subject, through themselves." Insofar as Auden enumerates "heterogeneous strings of things or people who are 'news'," he is a "journalist poet," but he is not "journalistic." "If the *Odyssey* is the work of a longshore Greek," argues MacNeice, "and *The Winding Stair* is the work of a crank philosopher, Auden's poems are the work of a journalist."

As his aesthetic principles developed MacNeice grew less enamored of journalism. Although he continued to believe that poets put "facts and feelings in italics," he grew disenchanted with those forms of imaginative writing which purport to be factual or objective. Having written his voluminous *Autumn Journal*—that extraordinary amalgam of public and private experience, confession and reportage—he could remark, in 1949, that he had tired of journalism. And by 1963, in the Clark Lectures that become *Varieties of Parable*, he had come to feel that the poet must restrain the journalist in himself. "In the 1930's we used to say that the poet should contain the journalist; now I would tend more often to use 'contain' in the sense of control or limit."

MacNeice had also wearied of realism. What had begun, in his Oxford years, as a wary attachment had ended in an amicable divorce. In his book on Yeats, MacNeice could say with confidence that "the poet's business is realism." Five years later, in his introduction to *The Dark Tower* (1946), a "parable play" for radio, he could say with equal assurance that "pure realism" was "almost played out." And seventeen years later, in *Varieties of Parable*, as he turned his attention to Spenser, Bunyan, Kafka, Beckett, Pinter, and Golding, he virtually dismissed the social realism of the Thirties, arguing that a fairy tale is "a much more solid affair than the average naturalistic novel, whose roots go little deeper than a gossip column."

Between those extremes lies no wavering mind but a high intelligence steering its way through the crosscurrents of modernism and the demands of the period for social consciousness. Like any sensitive writer of the Thirties, MacNeice felt the pressure to bring poetic imagination to bear upon social and political realities. While still an undergraduate at Oxford he wrote a paper attacking the extremes of "out-and-out 'realism'," on the one hand, and "out-and-out 'self-expression'" on the other. But he also felt a hunger, shared by his Oxford companions, for realism—or the romance of realism. "We wanted," as he later put it, "to play Hamlet in the shadow of the gas-works." That hunger persisted in MacNeice's writing of the Thirties, expressing itself in such coldly realistic poems as "Birmingham" and "Belfast" and, just as surely, in his early critiques of Eliot, Auden, and Yeats.

Initially, Eliot's brand of realism exhilarated MacNeice, but he later came to see the "squalor of Eliot" as a "romanticized squalor because treated, on the whole, rather bookishly as *décor*." Auden passed with somewhat higher marks. His *Paid on Both Sides* seemed to MacNeice to be "tragic where *The Waste Land* is defeatist, and realist where *The Waste Land* is literary." Tracing the growth of Yeats's realism, MacNeice found Synge's influence and Yeats's political involvement to be salutary, for both helped to save Yeats from Aestheticism. But Yeats was a special case:

> The normal poet—witness the Elizabethans—should not be afraid of touching pitch. But the pitch is so thick on the world thoroughfares nowadays that a poet needs exceptional strength not to stick in it. Yeats avoided the world thoroughfares. It would be a disaster if all poets were to imitate him. In his own case the great refusal was justified.

In MacNeice's own case, the great refusal came more gradually and much later. His poetic career was, in fact, the reverse of Yeats's, insofar as it began in realism and ended with a commitment to parable and fable. In *Modern Poetry* MacNeice contrasted the early "escapist" mode of Yeats with the realistic mode of the *New Signatures* poets, finding in the latter an "honest survey of the contemporary world" but also a "recognition of that world's potentialities for good." In Auden, Day-Lewis, and the others, he saw the promise of a poetry that could be both idealistic and realistic, "honest while taking sides."

Two years later, MacNeice was not so optimistic. While he had been writing his book on Yeats, World War II had broken out, and the distinction between escapist and realist art had lost much of its meaning:

> If the war made nonsense of Yeats's poetry and of all works that are called 'escapist', it also made nonsense of the poetry that professes to be 'realist.' My friends had been writing for years about guns and frontiers and factories, about the 'facts' of psychology, politics, science, economics, but the fact of war made their writing seem as remote as the pleasure dome in Xanadu. For war spares neither the poetry of Xanadu nor the poetry of pylons. . . . If war is the test of reality, then all poetry is unreal; but

in that case unreality is a virtue. If, on the other hand, war is a great enemy of reality, although an incontestable fact, then reality is something which is not exactly commensurable with facts.

The recognition stated here with a tone of revelation became, in subsequent years, a matter of conviction. Facts were not "reality"; nor was naturalism to be entrusted with the exploration of an "inner reality"—the thinghood of an object of event, the spiritual condition of a decade. "The single-track mind," argued MacNeice in 1946, "and the single-plane novel or play are almost bound to falsify the world in which we live." The presence of "fact in fantasy" and "method in madness"—a presence certified by Freudian psychology and confirmed by wartime events—demanded a "double-level" art, employing parable or allegory. And, as MacNeice turned in *The Dark Tower* and in his late poems to the mode of parable, so in his criticism he came to judge the works of his contemporaries not by their realism, in the narrow sense, but by their power to reveal the "inside of man" and the "inner feel" of the mid-century through the creation of "special worlds." Auden he found a "parabolist" but "not a consistent or sustained one." Eliot remained too much the Imagist to be a writer of parable. More instructive examples were to be found in Edwin Muir or in contemporary drama, particularly that of Beckett and Pinter.

MacNeice's long engagement with the problem of realism has a parallel in his protracted involvement with the issue of belief. In that struggle he was not, of course, alone. Valentine Cunningham, in *British Writers of the Thirties*, has chronicled the collapse of belief and the general loss, felt acutely by artists and writers of the Thirties, of a "religious and intellectual order that would make sense of things." Yet even among intellectuals of the period, MacNeice's case is extreme, his position more ambiguous than most. D.B. Moore (in *The Poetry of Louis MacNeice*) sees in MacNeice's skepticism a "moral failure," an inability to "achieve faith, deny all belief, or to systematize his agnosticism." By contrast, Terence Brown (in *Louis MacNeice: Sceptical Vision*) finds a rigorous "sceptical faith, which believes that no transcendent reality, but rather non-being, gives being value." And William McKinnon (in *Apollo's Blended Dream*) sees in MacNeice's outlook "a deep and abiding awareness of the poet's need for belief," together with an awareness of a need to find "the forms, especially the tone of voice, appropriate to the creative expression of that belief." Where these conflicting opinions agree is in their recognition of MacNeice's skepticism, his resistance to cynicism, and his persistent search for the grounds of belief. "When I went up to Oxford," he recalls, "I felt hampered by [the] lack of belief. . ." That feeling persisted until the end of his life, giving urgency to his poetry and a demanding edge to his literary criticism.

To the two most compelling belief-systems of the Thirties, those of Communism and Catholicism, MacNeice could offer sympathy but no commitment. MacNeice has sometimes been linked with Leftist writers of the Thirties, but a more accurate description may be found in *British Writers of the Thirties*, where Cunningham groups MacNeice with other "refuseniks" of the period, including Orwell, Isherwood, and Dylan Thomas. In his poetry MacNeice does not take sides, and in his prose he most often strikes the stance of detached observer, who reports (in *I Crossed the Minch*) that he once fell asleep on a train while reading Day-Lewis's Leftist essays, or looks with a piercing eye on Marxian utopias:

> No doubt [Yeats and Eliot] were also influenced by ulterior, that is personal, motives; each wanted a world in which he, as an intellectual, could live. The left wing intellectual, before he throws a stone at them, should consider whether his own motives for advocating 'the classless society' are disinterested. I have a suspicion that many intellectuals of the Left fancy this society with a special niche for themselves in it, that they take it the writer will be honoured when the banker and the aristocrat have gone. . .

It is significant that in criticizing the Leftist intelligentsia

MacNeice should allude to a Biblical parable about throwing stones. The son of an Anglican bishop, MacNeice was haunted by formal religion, and as Edna Longley has shown (in *Louis MacNeice: A Study*), Biblical images and cadences often inform his poems. Yet MacNeice could not follow Eliot and Graham Greene into an acceptance of Christian dogma, nor could he accompany Auden into overt political commitment. He remained an island to himself, suspicious on the one hand of Leftist ideology but unable on the other to return to his father's faith.

Nonetheless, MacNeice continued to defend the marriage of poetry and politics and to value religious belief, not only as spiritual nourishment but as a matter of aesthetic principle. "Major poetry usually implies a belief," he declares in *Modern Poetry*, adding that a poet's beliefs must be "compromised" by observation. "To shun dogma does not mean to renounce belief," he remarks in "The Poet in England Today" (1940), while sharply distinguishing propaganda from belief. And in his introduction to *The Dark Tower* he ventures an absolute:

> *The Faerie Queene*, *The Pilgrim's Progress*, *Piers Plowman*, and the early Moralities could not have been written by men without any beliefs. In an age which precludes the simple and militant faith of a Bunyan, belief (whether consciously formulated or not) still remains a *sine qua non* of the creative writer.

Belief is essential because, in MacNeice's view, it is a shaping principle in a work of art. It is integral to the making of a poem. MacNeice acknowledged that beliefs need not be "explicit" in a poem and warned against letting beliefs dominate a poetic text. But he strongly opposed I.A. Richards' severance of poetry from belief, on the grounds that "a poem flows from human life with which beliefs are inevitably entangled"; and he insisted that in many instances, such as that of Hopkins, belief is "structurally essential." In *Varieties of Parable* he describes beliefs as "formalizing elements," which "have a part in the shaping of [a] poem," and he suggests that the act of making a poem may bring the poet back to "something very like belief—rather as if God . . . when he looked at his work and saw that it was good, had found himself forced to believe in himself."

In his practical criticism, MacNeice often raises the issue of belief. Reflecting on modern drama, he laments the loss of its religious function. Eulogizing Dylan Thomas, he praises the poet's "faith in something that is simultaneously physical and spiritual." And lambasting Yeats, he argues that the poet's "belief in belief" turned him into a poseur. But rarely does MacNeice challenge or judge a poet's beliefs. Rather, he contends that a belief is good if it is right for the poet—that is, if it strengthens the poetry:

> Yeats, like Gerard Manley Hopkins, was a special case. Those critics are fools who lament that, if Hopkins had not been a Jesuit, he would have written much better poetry. If Yeats had been different from what he was, if he had had different beliefs, or even been capable of different beliefs, he might not have written at all.

Nor does MacNeice attempt to prove or disprove his contemporaries' beliefs. His intent is more often to examine them—and to approach, through the act of criticism, a definition of his own skeptical position.

II

HOWEVER SPECULATIVE his turn of mind, Louis MacNeice wrote from a poet's standpoint. He had little interest in theories of poetry and scant patience with critics who grind theoretical axes at the expense of individual poems. A poet's generalizations, he argued, are to be accepted only as "dramatic": as a "moment in the context of a poet's life and work." And though he exemplified fair-mindedness, he disclaimed objectivity. "I do not, therefore, profess to attempt a reasoned, balanced, objective, or historical criticism of my contemporaries."

What he attempted instead was personal criticism, grounded in the values of classicism but open to unconventional modes and forms. For all his metaphysical uncertainty, MacNeice was not lacking in aesthetic criteria—or free of literary prejudice. He disapproved of esoteric subjects, obscurity, incoherence, the "sloppiness" of Surrealism, the trivialities of Imagism, and the "purely cerebral jigsaw writing" of William Empson. He favored rhyme, meter, musicality, and suppleness of line, but he also relished a poetic voice with "an echo of the traffic in it." In his own poems he sought a "controlled flamboyance" of diction, and in the language of his contemporaries he looked for similar qualities:

> Our diction must have vigour, be familiar enough to be recognizable, new enough to be arresting. But vigour at the cost of lucidity or sincerity or proportion is to be avoided.

A poet's diction should be "masculine but not exhibitionist." It should reflect a balance of energy and classical restraint.

MacNeice's biases enlivened his criticism, as did his sometimes devastating rationality, his agile and surgical logic. Although he was seldom overtly malicious, he excelled in both the pithy—or scathing—phrase and the extended, withering analysis. When dull American Joyceans come to Dublin, he remarked, they can't tell the "wind in the reeds from the tongue in the cheek." Oxford specializes in "soft-spoken malice," "heavy-lidded thin-lipped irony," an "addiction to verbal arabesques," and the "exquisite verdigris of cynicism." Yeats is "too much the tragedian ever to become a pessimist"; Eliot's humour is "the humour of a don"; and Housman is "the English Romantic masochistically practicing heroics in the last ditch." Beyond such quips and *apercus*, MacNeice offered reasoned analysis, as incisive in its way as his aphoristic thrusts. Having entertained Yeats's argument that "art is not for the crowd," he points to two "amusing inconsistencies" in Yeats's logic:

> First, having just declared himself an enemy of *popular* literature, he seems oddly interested in the opinions which "all men" are

going to accept or reject. Secondly, while implicitly attacking Matthew Arnold, he is at the same time accepting Arnold's view of the arts as man's only means of communication with eternity. When Arnold used the term "criticism of life" he meant not surface comment but the demonstration of the Universals which lie beneath the particular. Yeats on the contrary writes here as if the Universals were cut off from us in some transcendent world of their own, like the gods of Epicurus.

By such measures MacNeice kept his distance from Yeats's social hierarchies, Eliot's aesthetic dogmas, and Auden's political allegiances.

Yet MacNeice also immersed himself in the work of those poets, and though his criticism ranged widely, pursuing interests as diverse as Aeschylus, George Herbert, Seferis, Joyce, Irish legend, O'Casey, and Austin Clarke, it recurred often to the three literary giants who, in very different ways, mattered the most to MacNeice and his contemporaries.

"For me the history of post-War poetry in England," wrote MacNeice, "is the history of Eliot and the reaction from Eliot." With other poets of his generation MacNeice found himself reacting not only to Eliot's example but also to the force of his critical doctrines, particularly those set down in his essay on the Metaphysical poets and in "Tradition and the Individual Talent." Reading Eliot's early poems at the age of eighteen, MacNeice found them repellent and obscure. Not long afterward, however, he came to admire their contemporary subject-matter—their cigarette butts and smells of steak in passageways. In Eliot's most serious poems, MacNeice observed, "common or squalid objects took on a massiveness," evoking what Eliot called the boredom and the glory of daily life. Yet, as noted above, MacNeice later came to regard Eliot's "realism" as spurious, a matter of props and decor. And in *Modern Poetry* he rendered this tempered verdict:

I still think of the earlier Eliot as the poet of cigarette stubs—not a great poet nor essentially a tragic poet, but a very sensitive aesthete in literature, learned in and obsessed with the past, for whom the problem is not the problem of a world-builder or a believer or a rebel or even a reporter, but the problem of a rather pedantic individualist who would like his daily life and his personal relationships to conform to some pattern which he has extracted from other people's poetry or philosophy. But that conformity is unachieveable and so he sits blowing smoke-rings.

Eliot's pronouncements elicited an equally measured response. The Old Possum's self-proclaimed classicism left MacNeice—a trained classicist—unmoved. In Eliot's poems he found a classical economy of statement and precision of image, but the dominant tone, he argued, was softly romantic—a blend of nostalgia, self-pity, and swagger under disguise. Eliot's theory of impersonality, as articulated in "Tradition and the Individual Talent," had even less meaning for MacNeice, for in practice, he remarked, it amounted to little more than Eliot's avoiding saying "I." In Eliot's celebrated statement that poetry amalgamates thoughts of Spinoza with the noise of the typewriter and the smell of cooking, MacNeice found an expression of empiricism—and a description of Eliot's own limitations:

> Eliot is a person of exceptional book-learning, for whom . . . an idea is really an experience and who does tend to bring in Spinoza when he hears the noise of the typewriter . . . I suspect that Eliot is bound to be a rather esoteric poet because. . . he really is more interested in ideas on the one hand and sense-impressions on the other—Spinoza and smells—than in concrete life or the concrete human being.

Similarly, Eliot's dictum that a modern poem must be difficult struck MacNeice as inadvertent self-description. "It is not wrong of Eliot to be difficult," he remarked, "because Eliot would be posing if he were easy." Eliot's poems are difficult, in part, because they "over-work images with private significance" and because Eliot "will not commit himself; and the world cannot understand people who will not commit themselves." But it is specious to extend Eliot's self-description to poetry in general—even poetry that attempts, as Eliot put it, to comprehend the variety and complexity of modern civilization. MacNeice concurred with Empson in believing that poetry is essentially ambiguous, but "ambiguity is not necessarily obscure." Contrasting the poets of *New Signatures* with Eliot, he found in the former a model of complexity joined to lucidity. But it is "wrong to go out of one's way to be intelligible. The poet must fulfill (a far better word than 'express') himself."

To the question of Eliot's style and its influence on younger poets, MacNeice had a similarly mixed response. Although he disapproved of the "collage-method" of *The Waste Land*, finding it "heterogeneous and therefore bad," he acknowledged Eliot's mastery of the "startling but inevitable image," his bonding of image and rhythm, his precise control of nuance and mood. What is most striking in Eliot, he observed, is his "gift for point and his surprise effects." But "point and surprise can both be faked"; and in the later poems, particularly *Burnt Norton*, some of Eliot's effects seemed to MacNeice to ring false, Eliot's style having "hardened into a kind of mannerism of antithesis or oxymoron." Among the techniques MacNeice admired were Eliot's blend of conversation and incantation, his "so-called free association," his "deliberate flatness," his quick cinematic cuts, his delicate syntax, and his supple expressive line. And despite MacNeice's objection to *The Waste Land* as a model, he found Eliot's general influence to be beneficial, insofar as it widened the range of poetic subject-matter and promoted rigor and precision in younger poets. Whatever its worth as a model, *The Waste Land* remained for MacNeice a profound achievement, for "to have painted the Waste Land so precisely that those who had never to their conscious knowledge been there could so fully recognize it . . . was the feat of a great poet."

In Wystan Auden, MacNeice encountered another formidable contemporary, whose influence was equal to Eliot's but far more personal. During the Thirties Auden and MacNeice were close friends and traveling companions, and throughout his career MacNeice, like Spender and Day-Lewis, remained in Auden's shadow. In "The Oxford Boys Becalmed" (1937) Edmund Wilson complains that MacNeice, "the most gifted of the Auden group, the master of a lyric impressionism that differs from the work of the rest, appears . . . to have toppled over on Auden and to have become almost indistinguishable from him." More recently, Valentine Cunningham has heard the voice of Auden in MacNeice's epithets and in such lines as "The even tenor of the usual day." Never mind that the line also sounds like Thomas Gray. Since the Thirties MacNeice's critics have been determined to see him as good but derivative—a pleasant valley in the Land of Auden.

Given this ego-corrosive climate of opinion, MacNeice's criticism of Auden is remarkably sympathetic—and remarkably impartial. Between 1931 and 1940 MacNeice reviewed Auden's major collections, praising their achievement while warning against certain tendencies of style. Most often his critiques focus on subject-matter and techniques, commending Auden's versatility, inclusiveness, and technical innovation. Such flaws as he finds are usually the obverse of Auden's virtues.

"Auden's great asset is curiosity," MacNeice remarks in "Poetry Today" (1935). "[W]hat I especially admire in you," he reaffirms in "Letter to W.H. Auden" (1937) "is your unflagging curiosity about people and events." Contrasting Auden with Eliot, MacNeice characterizes Auden as a vibrant poet living in a concrete world. "Unlike Eliot, he is not (as a poet) tired. . . . he is not old with reading the Fathers. He reads the newspapers and samples ordnance maps. He has . . . the gusto which comes from an unaffected (almost ingenuous) interest in people, politics, careers, science, psychology, landscape and mere sensations." Those attributes have broadened Auden's range far beyond that of most lyric poets, admitting Freudian theory, economics, and politics, on the one hand, and lightness, frivolity, and vulgarity, on the other. Auden's curiosity has given him "something to write *about*." And his felicitous impurity, his willingness to "lump the vulgarity," to write light verse and incorporate the rhythms of the music hall, have imparted a warmth not to be found in Eliot. By his inclusiveness he has done justice to "the multiplicity of life"; and in his willingness to include "unpoetic" subject-matter, to abandon high-mindedness for earthy directness, he has "brought back humanity into English poetry."

MacNeice regarded Auden as less sophisticated than Eliot, technically and intellectually, but he also found in Auden's poems a rich variety and a mastery of certain idiosyncratic techniques. "Mr. Auden's attempt," he wrote of *Poems* (1930), "is to put the soul across in telegrams." Auden's omission of minor parts of speech appealed to MacNeice, as did the use of "dream technique":

> When I say that Auden uses a dream technique, I mean for instance that he is very fond of that figure which Aristotle classes as a species of metaphor—the particular standing for the general. As in the dream, if porpoises are mentioned, I do not think of porpoises in general or of 'porpoiseness', but may even see a particular porpoise crystallize out of nothing. Hence Auden's notorious catalogues.

Beyond this central, definitive technique, MacNeice identified some fourteen "tricks in Auden and his fellows," among them counterpointed rhythm, false rhyme, "broken or accelerated syntax," assonance, omitted capitals at the beginning of lines, and "pauses (mental and metrical)." For the most part MacNeice approved of those techniques while recognizing that in the work of Auden's followers they had sometimes been abused.

As for flaws in Auden's own poems, MacNeice found nothing more troubling than lapses of taste and minor deficiencies of style. Reviewing *On the Frontier*, MacNeice confessed that the mystical love scenes "made one long for a sack to put one's head in." Less caustically, he questioned Auden's satiric use of ballad form and warned against writing down to the crowd. He also noted Auden's "slapdash" methods of composition, his excessive use of slant rhyme, his deployment of scientific jargon, and his sacrifice of lucidity "for the sake of concentration and pattern." But these were forgivable imperfections in a poet who had, in MacNeice's judgment, helped to restore heroic values to modern poetry, and who had demonstrated "more vitality than all his fellow-poets put together." In one of his last reviews of Auden, a piece on *Another Time* (1940), MacNeice pronounced his friend and rival "the most gifted and the most exciting poet of his generation."

MacNeice had similar things to say of W.B. Yeats, though he tempered his enthusiasm with stern detachment. Explaining why he undertook a booklength study of Yeats, MacNeice remarked that he found the older poet strange enough to excite his interest but "near enough to me myself to preclude my misrepresenting him too grossly." That balance undergirds *The Poetry of W.B. Yeats*, lending MacNeice's remarks uncommon authority. Whether he is discussing Yeats's emerging realism, or tracing the influence of Ireland on Yeats's verse, or decrying Yeats's "belief in belief," MacNeice maintains the tone of the informed observer, whose purpose is to show that Yeats, "granted his limitations, was a rich and complex poet, who often succeeded by breaking his own rules and who turned his own liabilities into assets."

"If Auden had written poems about the Rosses," MacNeice remarked, "he would never have left out the Metal Man who stands in the harbour." Thus MacNeice epitomizes the differences between Yeats and Auden—or, more broadly, between Yeats's late aestheticism and the social realism of the Auden-Spender school. Those differences color MacNeice's remarks on Yeats's realism, or lack of it, particularly with respect to the earlier poems. MacNeice takes issue with Spender's snide dismissal of "The Lake Isle of Innisfree" as a poem which "calls up the image of a young man reclining on a yellow satin sofa." But he notes the lack of "timber" in Yeats's early poems, and he chronicles with approval Yeats's development from dreamy languor to "hard statement," self-pity to anger, and tender escapism to the tough-minded realism of "September 1913" and "Easter 1916." From MacNeice's standpoint, Yeats's experience of public life and Irish politics, his role in the controversies of the Abbey Theatre, and his thwarted courtship of Maud Gonne bestowed a belated grace. Compelling Yeats "to have truck with humanity," they spared him the fate of other Nineties aesthetes, who clung to the "feminine," rarified world of Pater and were lost thereby.

Yeats's quarrels with unromantic Ireland, voiced most vehemently in "September 1913," held particular interest for MacNeice. With Yeats, MacNeice felt a profound ambivalence toward "the land of ambush, / Purblind manifestoes, never-ending complaints, / The born martyr and the gallant ninny" (*Autumn Journal*, XVI). Moreover, in Yeats's *Autobiographies* he found a mirror of his own childhood:

> When I read Yeats's account of his childhood I find many things which are echoed in my own or in that of other Irish people I know—in particular, the effects of loneliness . . . the clannish obsession with one's own family; the combination of anarchist individualism with puritanical taboos and inhibitions; the half-envious contempt for England; the constant desire to show off; a sentimental attitude to Irish history; a callous indifference to those outside the gates; an identification of Ireland with the spirit and of England with crass materialism.

MacNeice also found common ground in certain Irish traits and certain features of the Irish landscape. The Irish, he observed, are "born puritans" and "born partisans." But at the root of the Irish character lies a "set of antinomies": the sentimental and the unsentimental; the personal and the impersonal; the "slapdash" and the formal. Those antinomies shape Yeats's poems, as does the presence of the Irish landscape:

An Irish landscape is capable of pantomimic transformation scenes; one moment it will be desolate, dead, unrelieved monotone, the next it will be an indescribably shifting pattern of prismatic light. . . .

Yeats's best-known landscapes were Sligo and Galway, and he deliberately set out to match his verse to them. I do not think it fanciful to maintain that he succeeded, that there is something palpably in common between the subtle colour and movement of his verse and that western landscape which is at the same time delicate and strong.

Like Yeats, MacNeice had roots in the West of Ireland. Whatever its merits as literary criticism, this passage expresses a shared love of the landscape and a strong sense of affinity between the two poets.

Where they parted company was on the issue of belief. As portrayed by MacNeice, Yeats was at heart a lifelong skeptic—a nonbeliever who willed himself to believe in dubious doctrines and who tailored facts to accommodate his beliefs. Under the influence of Pater, Yeats came to believe in the supremacy of passion. Under the influence of theosophy he came to believe in the mystical doctrines of Rosicrucianism, without having had the mystical experiences that might corroborate such beliefs. When compared to Rilke's thought, MacNeice observed, Yeats's "would-be dogmas and stock symbols look gimcrack." For Rilke "had had genuine mystical experiences where Yeats, in all probability, had only wished to have them." Similarly, Yeats's vaunted Anglo-Irish heritage was little more than a polite fiction—and another instance of Yeats's wish-fulfilling fakery:

Owing . . . to a belief in aristocracy he faked a legend about his family. Owing to a belief in mysticism he pretended to mystical experience. Owing to a belief in Ireland he—at times—misrepresented her. His distortions of fact . . . were accounted for by a belief; believing that things ought to be so, he wrote as if they were so.

Yet, despite his demonstrable fraudulence and (in the eyes of Auden) his intellectual silliness, Yeats remained for MacNeice's generation a model of the serious modern poet. "[I]t was Yeats's *dryness* and *hardness* that excited us," MacNeice recalls, enumerating among Yeats's salient modern virtues his widening of subject-matter, his exploration of moral and philosophical problems, his dealings with contemporary experience, and his knack (as A.E. put it) for making common speech aristocratic. Citing "No Second Troy," MacNeice applauded Yeats's "peculiar gift of making something memorable and even sensuous out of ordinary words, austere rhythms and statements bleakly direct." Elsewhere he praises Yeats's mastery of the non-stanzaic short-line poem (such as "The Fisherman") and his ability "so to control the rhythms that the poem does not get into a skid." Such mastery inspired MacNeice and his contemporaries, who could emulate Yeats's prowess while rejecting his attitudes and doctrines. "The spiritual lesson that my generation . . . can learn from Yeats," concluded MacNeice, "is to write according to our lights. His lights are not ours. *Go thou and do otherwise.*"

III

Twenty-seven years after his early death, Louis MacNeice remains alive in the memories of older writers. The late Howard Nemerov, who lunched frequently with MacNeice in the thirties, remembered him as a man of "genuine goodwill." John Montague has portrayed MacNeice as warm but taciturn, as "eminently approachable but ultimately lonely," an enthusiast of rugby matches who kept his own counsel, so much so that "only his women knew him well." Philip Booth remembers MacNeice as an "immensely nice man" and recalls his visit to Dartmouth in the early fifties, where MacNeice quoted in conversation W.R. Rodgers' remark that a poem is "a party to which you invite all the words you know." To which MacNeice added, with characteristic charm, "the real fun is how they pair off, who goes home with whom." Such sparkling moments linger in the memories of MacNeice's survivors, though Montague also describes him as one whom "melancholy had marked for her own"; and Stephen Spender (in his *Washington Diary*, 1965) recalls with some disdain how MacNeice would lean back against a wall, "regarding one with amused detachment through half-closed eyes."

It is an open question whether MacNeice's literary reputation remains so vividly alive. Here the signs are ambiguous and conflicting. A few years ago, the University of Liverpool hosted a conference honoring MacNeice, and a new edition of his *Selected Poems*, edited by Michael Longley, has been issued jointly by Faber and Wake Forest University Press. In Northern Ireland MacNeice has garnered sustained attention, both as a poet in his own right and as a father-figure for such younger poets as Paul Muldoon. Yet one can look far and wide before finding a collection of MacNeice, new or used, in Dublin—a place he rightly described as "never my town." And in this country, there are educated readers who know MacNeice only as an adjunct of Auden, or as a minor poet of the Thirties. That he also wrote first-rate criticism is scarcely known at all.

The survival of that criticism will, I suspect, depend on more than its intrinsic merits. "He never published a word that is not good reading," T.S. Eliot said in his obituary; but one wonders whether MacNeice's critical books, which have not been readily available, will ever have the audience they deserve. As a critic MacNeice had blind spots and shortcomings, among them his limited sympathy with American poetry, his bias toward public subject-matter, his contempt for Surrealism, his preoccupation with technique, his debunking attitude toward mysticism, and his lack of interest in women poets, whom he rarely even mentions. But for those who will read him, MacNeice offers humane exacting criticism and a practitioner's insights into the art. Audacious as they sometimes are, his critiques show a deep respect for fellow poets and a reverence for an art which he regarded as "one of the chief embodiments of human dignity." And, however dated it may be, his critical writing—addressed more often to a general audience than to academics—is a refreshing change from the theory-laden, jargon-infested prose that clogs our academic journals.

Moreover, it is no exaggeration to say that in his literary judgments MacNeice was more often right than wrong—or often more right than wrong. His view of Eliot's "impersonality" has, I believe, become accepted opinion, as has his view of Yeats's putative lineage, and much more. And even when MacNeice was dead wrong, he could be as provocative as Samuel Johnson writing on Thomas Gray or Edmund Wilson writing on Eliot. Commenting on Stephen Spender in "Poetry Today" (1935), MacNeice remarked:

> He will . . . be the man for posterity, if our poetry is ever dug up in fragments; here is someone who really *felt*, posterity will say; and will conclude that he died young.

To those of us who write criticism, it is heartening to find that so prescient a critic could, for once, be so wide of the mark.

1990

Revisiting The Bell

In October, 1940, Seán O'Faoláin and Peadar O'Donnell launched a monthly magazine, which they chose to call *The Bell*. "Any other equally spare and hard and simple word would have done," O'Faoláin explained, "any word with a minimum of associations" (10/40, 1).[1] Based in Dublin, *The Bell* was to be a new magazine for a new nation. It was to nurture and mirror the growth of Éire—an eighteen-year-old nation with a long memory, an uncertain identity, and many myths to shed. Over the next fourteen years, the magazine surpassed its founders' expectations, attracting writers of the stature of Elizabeth Bowen, Sean O'Casey, George Bernard Shaw, and Louis MacNeice and becoming the most prominent Irish journal of its time. An outspoken critic of the Catholic hierarchy, the government, and the Gaelic League, it also became a force for social reform, engendering respect and outrage on both sides of the border.

During one of my sojourns in Ireland I had heard about *The Bell* and knew something of its distinguished reputation. So when I saw a listing, some years ago, for sixty-two back issues of the magazine in a catalogue from Kenny's Bookshops in Galway, I

---

[1] Numbers in parentheses indicate month, year, and page. A generous and judicious selection of work from *The Bell* may be found in *The Best from* The Bell, edited by Sean McMahon (O'Brien, 1978). I am indebted to McMahon's scholarship.

called to order them. Without so much as a credit-card number, Mr. Desmond Kenny agreed to send them by the next post, and not long afterward, my sixty-two issues arrived, most of them in remarkably good condition. Each had the heft and look of a volume of poems. Their cover design, a simple diamond pattern in a single solid color, bespoke an appealing candor. As I turned the pages of those fragile issues, with their speckled wartime paper, their ads for Pye Radios and Sunbeam Wolsey Underwear, their stories by Frank O'Connor, Liam O'Flaherty, and Mary Lavin, I looked forward to some fine reading and perhaps some insight into the period.

As it turned out, I was in for a good bit more than superior entertainment. For what I had bought, sight unseen, were some four thousand pages of fact and opinion, trenchant prose and stately polemic, hard-edged fiction and courageous social journalism. Under the editorial hand of O'Faoláin (1940-46) and later of O'Donnell (1946-54), *The Bell* offered its readers a potpourri of poems, personal essays, articles, book reviews, short stories, literary appreciations, historical reflections, and incisive political analysis. A typical issue opened with a 3,000-word editorial, wherein the stupidity of the "Gaelic cult" or the pieties of Eamon de Valera or the complacencies of the bourgeoisie came under vehement attack. It closed with a popular column entitled "The Open Window," in which Michael Farrell, a supple stylist who wrote under the pseudonym Gulliver, conducted a "monthly perambulation," entertaining whatever topics crossed his mind.

"This is your magazine," declared O'Faoláin in his inaugural editorial. "[T]his is not so much a magazine as a bit of Life itself, and we believe in Life, and leave Life to shape us after her own image and likeness" (10/40). As originally conceived, *The Bell* was to be a "survey of Irish life." Potential contributors were invited to report on their experiences, dispensing with generalizations and abstractions, which are "the luxury of people who enjoy befuddling themselves methodically." The editors sought "bits of individual veracity, hidden in the dust-heaps of convention, imitation, timidity, traditionalism, wishful thinking." The doors were open to anyone—"Gentile or Jew, Protestant or Catholic, priest or layman, Big House or Small House"—who could present "Life before any abstraction" and could illuminate "some corner of life that nobody else can know." Only "lunatics" and "sour-bellies" would be excluded.

After only a year of publication, the editors found their course in need of correction. Life, they discovered, could be "sadly inarticulate," and the early pieces on such topics as Street Ballads, Poaching, and Cottage Furniture, often written by amateurs, had needed heavy editing. Moreover, the plain people of Ireland, they came to feel, needed education, prodding, and chiding as much as a day in court. Although O'Faoláin never lost his "humble respect for Irish brains," by mid-decade *The Bell* had developed a relationship with its community—and with a readership estimated at 30,000—that was as often adversarial as exploratory. Significantly, in March, 1945, two epigraphs appeared on the editorial page, one from Corneille ("Du ciel de sa Providence infinie, / Dieu a donné à chaque peuple un différent genie") and one from Socrates ("God has placed us upon this great city like a hornet upon a noble horse to sting it and keep it awake"). If the first reaffirmed the magazine's fascination with cultural identity, the second proclaimed its role as caustic social critic. Whether they be Celtophiles or Anglophobes, puritans or chauvinists, "Little Irelanders" or the "stuffed shirts" of the bureaucracy, those who would betray the national ideals or prevent Ireland from realizing her full potential were given fair warning.

If one may judge from contemporary accounts, such people were not in short supply. Nor has any post-colonial country been more in need of nurture and renewal. The commentator who observed the shadow of the Great Famine over midcentury Ireland may have been hallucinating, but there were certainly shadows of more recent memory, among them the atrocities of the Black and

Tans and the fratricides of the Irish civil war. Since 1929 there had been the deathly shadow of censorship, under which, as O'Faoláin observed, "[p]ractically every Irish writer of note [had] at one time or another been. . . in the interests of the most unsophisticated banned in his own country" (1/47, 23). And there was the more diffuse cloud of Ireland's wartime neutrality, which reinforced its geographical insularity and strengthened an indigenous isolationism. In a scathing letter to the editor, one V. McGuire of 15 Pembroke Park, Dublin, lamented his country's spiritual condition:

> One wonders whether Ireland is always going to be a backward island on the fringes of Europe, meandering through the centuries in self-imposed isolation, in a fog of smug self-satisfaction, while the best of her people distinguish themselves for valour, culture and skill in other lands. The young, the vigorous and the enterprising cannot content themselves with a life without scope and opportunity. If they do not find these things at home they will inevitably depart and just as inevitably stay away. Ask any graduate of our Universities, ask any worker. You will get the same answer. They will not return (11/45).

Elsewhere, Michael Farrell responded with resignation to a report that a schoolboy had been caned for using the word "body" in an essay. "There was a time," Farrell sighed, "when this story would have angered and disgusted me. But the sword wears out its sheath and the heart wears out the breast, and, in Ireland, one must rest" (10/43, 85).

Not everyone was so resigned, least of all O'Faoláin, who tried, on the one hand, to locate centers of vitality in his dormant nation, and, on the other, to generate intellectual debate. That dual purpose gave impetus and direction to the early issues of *The Bell*, which presented symposia on a variety of national issues, articles on such subjects as ceilidhes and turf-cutting, short stories in the vein of Irish realism, and cosmopolitan editorials under the heading of "One World." Like most major Irish writers, O'Faoláin had spent extended time away from Ireland; but unlike most, he had returned in 1933 to what he called his "old, small, intimate, and much-trodden country," where he was to live for the rest of his life. If he sought, in part, to show Ireland as it truly was, and to ferret out signs of life wherever they might be found, he also sought to rattle the civil servants and to harry a reluctant populace into the twentieth century.

Among the means employed in the early issues, the most ambitious were O'Faoláin's symposia, which sometimes ran for several months, incorporating readers' responses. One of the most informative, entitled "The Five Strains" (9/41), presented historical discussions of the Gaelic, Norman, Classical, Anglo-Irish, and English components of Irish culture. One of the boldest, entitled "The Creeds," invited statements from representatives of the Catholic, Anglican, Presbyterian, Unitarian, Quaker, and Jewish faiths. And one of the most provocative, a forum on censorship, presented a muddled "defence" of censorship by Monk Gibbon, followed by rebuttals from some of Ireland's leading writers. Arguing that censorship protected the young, and that Strindberg ("that life-hating neurotic") *deserved* to be banned, Gibbon drew a cool dismissive breeze from George Bernard Shaw, who conceded that "a civilization of free-booters is impossible," and a fierce blast from Sean O'Casey, who denounced Gibbon's argument as a "comic medley of fright, fear, superstition, faint piety, greek fire, and a cool desire to keep on the lee side of the counts, knights, and esquires of the Holy Roman Empire" (2/45, 401). O'Casey also claimed that the U.S.S.R. had never banned a book, and he celebrated Joyce as "the bravest and finest soul in literature Ireland has had for many years."

Commendable though they are, O'Faoláin's symposia have an academic tone that seems discordant with the demotic spirit of *The Bell*. More in keeping with that spirit, the essayists teased out the secrets of the trades and the energies of the vernacular, finding beauty and humor in unlikely places. In "Big Mine-

Shooting," Patrick Campbell, an officer in the Port Control Service, narrates a droll account of defusing drifting mines in Dublin Bay, explaining that "the way most people feel about mines is this: after the circuit has been broken and the acid removed and the detonator and explosive charge taken out and buried the mine is going to go off immediately. It is an attitude that earns no ribbons on the chest, but there will be no wax flowers in glass bowls either" (5/43, 108). In "A Country Bookshop," Bryan MacMahon recounts the experience of managing a bookstore in Listowel:

> One country girl spent an hour disgruntedly throwing the contents of my trays over and over and examining only the 'holy ones.' 'Why,' I exclaimed at last with rapidly diminishing store of patience, 'there's one that'd be ideal for a priest.' 'Ach, man,' she replied, 'will you houl your tongue, 'tis for a bishop I want it' (3/41, 11).

And in one of the most popular pieces ever to appear in *The Bell*, a serial narrative entitled "I Did Penal Servitude," a provincial banker convicted of embezzlement recalls his experience in the Mountjoy and Portlaoighise prisons, where he found most of the inmates to be healthy, well-read men, long on decency but short on self-esteem. His unembellished narrative, which later became a best-seller in Ireland, ends with a poignant sketch of an ex-felon's re-entry into society:

> A man who will be a Convict on ticket-of-leave for two more years and then will be branded an 'ex-convict' for the rest of his life in a country where everybody can trace their neighbour's antecedents for three generations, I fear his real punishment is only beginning; round every corner Life has 'three days' bread and water' waiting for him (3/45, 523).

The note of social protest sounded in "Penal Servitude" grew louder as *The Bell* evolved. During the early years of the magazine, its personal essayists entertained such subjects as dance halls, swing music, and the arrival of jazz in Ballyjamesduff, often writing in a bemused or ironic tone. But by the mid-forties its journalists were taking on such controversial matters as unemployment, educational reform, the fate of the Irish language, the rights of women, and the shame of the Dublin slums, and the tone had grown more strident. In "A Plea from the Country" (6/46) Hubert Butler deplored the neglect of folk traditions and called for a state-sponsored museum of history and folklore, modeled after those in Scandinavia. In "Our School Readers" (10/46) William Glynn condemned the sentimental patriotism, bad verse, and nationalistic bias of the school textbooks, as well as the exclusion of such major authors as Synge, O'Flaherty, Shaw, and O'Faoláin. In "Women in Politics" (11/43) Hanna Sheehy-Skeffington observed that "[t]he party machine. . . is still male and still allergic to women," and in "Maids versus Mistresses" (10/43) Maura Laverty aired the grievances of chambermaids, including low wages and invasion of privacy. Contrasting the squalor of Dublin's slums with the government's denial of the problem, Sheila May bitterly remarked that only one change has occurred since independence: "The names of the alley and the street have been changed from English into Irish" (1/44, 356).

The hard-headed realism of those articles had its counterpart in *The Bell's* fiction, which tended to be short, Chekhovian, linear, and blunt. Under the censors' restrictions there was hardly a place for the likes of Henry Miller; and under the surveillance of O'Faoláin and O'Donnell, there was little room for surrealism, non-linear narrative, or experimental fiction. Bold as they could be in other matters, the editors favored conventionally structured stories that presented Irish life concretely, caught the rhythms of Irish speech, and looked with depth and understanding into the human heart, often finding a sense of shame. Having read more than a hundred stories in my sixty-two issues, I am struck by how many of them explore feelings of humiliation, particularly among Irish children and young adults. O'Faoláin's "Small Adam" (2/46) depicts a boy's humiliation at confession. Maeve Barrington's "Strong and Perfect Christians" (1/54) portrays a child's mortification on the eve of her first communion. Mary Lavin's "A Glimpse of Katey" (11/47) probes the loneliness and guilt of a child who fibs to her parents and must endure the consequences. At the other end of the life-span, Frank O'Connor's "The House that Johnny Built" (3/44) unfolds the comic, melancholy plight of a middle-aged bachelor, who twice proposes marriage and is twice turned down.

Those synopses may conjure a provincial *Dubliners*, but the favored style was seldom one of "scrupulous meanness." Its texture was earthier than that, its range of feeling warmer. And within the constraints of realism, Bryan MacMahon, James Plunkett, Seamus de Faoite, John Hewitt, and others found occasions for expansiveness and lyric flights. One very moving story, MacMahon's "The Good Dead in the Green Hills" (10/45), commemorates the death of the parish storyteller, who had earlier been relegated to the sidelines, his role usurped by the wireless. "[T]he radio and the story-teller made strange bedmates," the narrator observes; and the dignified funeral of Peadar Feeney, whose ancient stories had "the authenticity of immemorial age," signifies the passing of an older order:

> The following day all the people of the Lane mustered to the funeral. One man had left off drawing manure; another had given up grading eggs; another had ceased cutting turf in the bog outside the town; another had stopped plucking chickens in a fowl yard. Yet another had washed his bloodied hands in a butcher's porcelain trough as soon as he heard the dead bell banging out from the steeple . . . A hundred yards before us walked the priest, his white cypress catching all the light in the dull street. The blind man was directly in front of the coffin. I was in front of him again and he had his hand on my shoulder. Behind us I could hear the men changing fours frequently and even jostling subduedly for places under the coffin. That I knew as the best possible sign of a good funeral.

Infused with pathos but grittily realistic, MacMahon's story epitomizes the fiction published in *The Bell*. Looking both forward and backward, the author honors the Gaelic heritage while confronting the realities of social change.

That same tension enlivens O'Faoláin's eloquent editorials, which often upstage the performances of his contributors. By turns polemical, poetic, elegiac, witty, bitter, and monitory, the editors' monthly set-pieces have the weight if seldom the gravity of Johnson's moral essays. What gives them their enduring value is both their vigorous prose and their inherent drama: that of a metropolitan intellectual doing battle with sentimental nationalists, a realist poking a nation of groggy dreamers, a patriotic historian debunking a fraudulent mystique. In one of his angrier moments the editor exhorts his fellow writers "to keep hammering at such facts as that our children to-day are as hopeless putty in the hands of morons who have imposed on our generation a parody of an educational system beyond all description ignorant, narrow, and unrealistic, at which parents growl helplessly, at which the superiors of schools and convents can only wail and wring their hands, but in which the authors thereof obstinately and bearishly persist year after year against the protests of every class and creed . . ." (6/45, 205). Elsewhere, in a lighter vein, he likens the role of the intellectual in Éire to that of a ringmaster firing a man from a cannon:

> He must first say: 'Now, ladies and gentlemen, before I fire off this idea, I want everybody to be perfectly assured that there is absolutely *No Danger*. . . . What I am about to do is merely to make a very small and entirely safe . . . I cannot call it "explosion," I can only say a slight "percussion."

Continuing his reassurance, the ringmaster announces that the trajectory will be limited to fifty feet, that a safety net will be provided, and that, as a "final and careful consideration," he will fire "not a real live idea, but a dummy" (8/44, 374-5).

Using live ammunition, O'Faoláin trained his own cannon on the most stultifying forces in his society, chief among them the

"Gaelic cult," whose leaders had mythologized the Easter Rising, militantly institutionalized the Irish language, and promoted a vulgar Anglophobic nationalism. O'Faoláin expressed profound respect for Padraic Pearse, James Connolly, and other heroes of the 1916 rebellion. "Far be it from me," he wrote, "to assail the memory of brave and noble-hearted men whose courage and idealism we will for ever honor" (12/44, 192). As a social historian he understood the "natural and indeed . . . commendable eagerness to discover some thread of continuity that would lead us from the present to the past, tapping our deepest, most life-giving roots as a people . . ." (11/41, 98). The Gaelic language and literature, he acknowledged, were "like a well in whose dark silence one sees an image of that shadowy other-self which is our ancestral memory . . . Gaelic is essential if we wish to inform ourselves about ourselves" (5/42, 80-1). But the Gaelic League and its apostles had, in O'Faoláin's opinion, betrayed their own ideals; and what had begun as a revival of the "wild and fine spirit" of Gaelic culture had become, by 1940, an "enormous, ravelled, simple-minded web . . . of Gaelic Revivalism, stark Isolationism, timid and therefore savage Puritanism, crazy Censorship, all originally adumbrated on the highest moral motives, but alas, on the lowest intellectual level" (11/41, 103). Condemning the cult's uncritical worship of medieval Gaelic symbols, its weak grasp of Irish history, and its inefficacy as a revolutionary movement, he summoned his readers to awaken from the "very wonderful delusion" of Gaelic purity and face the facts of Irish history, among them the harsh fact that "the antique Gaels never heard of and would have fought to the death against the idea of a Republic and all it connotes, and the men who first initiated the idea of Republicanism—Tone onward—knew nothing about the antique Gaels and would . . . have been appalled by the reality of those days and conditions" (12/44, 191). Both the spirit of social revolution and the progress of modern Ireland have been impeded by the Gaelic mystique. "[D]rop the cult," O'Faoláin advised. "The course will be simple after that" (12/44, 196).

Of the principal architects of the Gaelic mystique, none was more central than Eamon de Valera, Taoiseach and later President of Éire, for whom O'Faoláin reserved his sharpest attacks. Socrates' hornet was never more in evidence than in the April, 1945 number, where the editor castigates the Taoiseach for a host of sins, including inaction, indecision, procrastination, lack of intellectual sophistication, and a benighted vision of national identity. As an opponent of the Free State and a fervent Republican, O'Faoláin had sided with de Valera during the civil war; and as the author of two biographies of the Taoiseach, he recognized his subject's personal virtues. But over the years O'Faoláin's attitude had shifted from admiration "this side idolatry" to acrid disaffection. "I believe myself that he is a good man," O'Faoláin acknowledged, "and he has, since his great days when he used to be a revolutionist, done very few wrong things, though chiefly because since then he has done very few practical things of any kind whatsoever" (4/45, 4). And de Valera's "masterly policy of inaction" had cost Ireland dearly:

> And so, we are constantly aware that thousands of our people have to be sent abroad to work, that thousands of them are probably lost to us for ever, that our slum problem is hardly being touched, that if the poor were not kept alive by doles of every kind many of them would simply starve to death, that it is only in the thirteenth year of office that the present Government introduces legislation to deal with tuberculosis, that our educational system is antediluvian, that we are in many respects a despotism disguised as a democracy, that the dismemberment of our country has been allowed to become a frozen problem, that our relations with Great Britain are as ambiguously unsatisfactory as they ever were (4/45, 18).

In its restrained intensity this indictment recalls Swift's Irish tracts. Here, as in his great predecessor, the tone is one of outrage tinged with despair.

Yet de Valera's inaction vexed O'Faoláin less than the Taoiseach's active role in matters of the spirit, namely his pro-

mulgating of a specious Irish identity. As the author of *The Irish*,
an historical meditation on the Irish character, O'Faoláin
deplored de Valera's equation of Ireland with the small farms of
the West and his reduction of Irish identity to its Gaelic, Catholic,
and southern components. "I can imagine no more stultifying and
stunting standard of living," wrote the editor, "or back-reference
than the Irish small farmer. Whether asleep or to all appearances
awake the small farmer follows an occupation which Shaw once
rightly called 'politically stupid and barely half-civilized,' and if
anybody, however much he may like the human qualities of the
peasant, should take his political standards from them he is com-
mitting intellectual hari-kiri" (4/45, 11). Nor should anyone take
his standards solely from the Catholic south. "Our Irishism is
only half-Irish without the Northern strain, just at the North is
only an artificial half-alive thing without the blood of Ireland run-
ning through its veins." O'Faoláin likened Partition to the man
who put a chicken's heart in a machine, where it went on beating
for years. "That is the North today. It is open to the North to
observe that our miracle of a chicken without a heart is even more
wonderful and less inspiring" (4/45, 7).

Countering de Valera, O'Faoláin envisioned a comprehensive
identity that would not only include the "five strains" but also
reaffirm the rebellious Gaelic spirit and the natural humanity of
the Irish people. In "Rebel by Vocation," an editorial on Wolfe
Tone, he praised the Anglo-Irish revolutionary, whom he regard-
ed as the father of modern Irish rebellion and the embodiment of
the Republican spirit. "We could do worse," he concluded, "than
go back to those beginnings" (11/46, 114). Likewise the new
urban middle class and the "stuffed shirts" of the civil service
could do worse than remember their rural origins. For the new
bourgeoisie had "lost all sense of its origins. The healthy, gener-
ous, humane sweep of feeling that we associate with the traditions
of our countryside no longer runs through society or political
life" (6/43, 189). In the Irish character O'Faoláin saw an "emol-

lient delicacy"—a "peasant kindness" whose roots lay in the harshness of rural life. Unlike de Valera, O'Faoláin did not idealize the small farmer or advocate a return to rural values. But he did urge a nurturing of that "emollient delicacy" and an honoring of its source: "Hardness as the father of softness. We shall never know what we owe to the wet sack on the shoulders, the dunging cow, the steam from the frieze pants before the fire" (11/45, 652).

Under O'Faoláin *The Bell* became, in part, a sustained study of the Irish character. For the editor, at least, that subject was inexhaustible. But from the beginning *The Bell* was also an outward-looking journal, which provoked its readers to look—and think—beyond their time and place. O'Faoláin was the first to recognize that "[i]n practice no man could live a full life of the spirit on cottage furniture, street ballads, or folk-lore, and we all . . . constantly feed body, mind, and spirit on the products and achievements of other countries and other times" (3/41, 5). In his "One World" editorials, his regular reports on political developments in Spain, the U.S.S.R., and other countries, and in his running critique of Irish parochialism, he promoted international awareness. In his September, 1944 editorial, after ruminating on the troubles of Austria, Serbo-Croatia, Lombardy, and Poland, he contrasted them with "our little troubles" and denounced the Irish "fixation" on local woes, which he compared to "a block in a petrol tube, stopping the engine of our natural human generosity from getting across to the rest of the world" (9/44, 471). Elsewhere, remarking upon the meaning of "Sinn Fein," he observed that "ourselves alone" had become "ourselves all alone," and that since independence Ireland had become escapist and timorous with respect to the rest of the world. "[P]olitical nationalism has . . . absolved us from the need for intelligent, constructive thought. The result has been that we have forgotten (if we ever knew) that ultimately every problem is not a problem of nationality but of civilization" (5/42, 77).

To counter such tendencies O'Faoláin, in his later editorials, offered not only his critiques of a blinkered nationalism but also his visions of a postwar world, a global community of "air warfare" and "swift communication," to which an old-fangled nationalism would be the sleepiest of responses. As a political pundit he could be wide of the mark, as when he assessed Soviet expansionism: "It is said that Russia can dominate Europe; even said that she already dominates the world . . . Who knows enough about Russia to say that she either could or really wants to?" (5/45, 104). But his purpose was not so much to augur the future as to propel his country into entering the new world order. "Our capacity to balance our duty *to Ireland*," he argued, "and our *duty to Ireland as part of the world* will . . . not merely measure our worth and dignity as a people, but it may well measure our success and achievement" (5/45, 106). And what might be the alternative to Ireland's joining the world? In one of his last editorials, he imagined the worst. "Could Ireland vanish? The world is dotted with the trails of aborted cultures, the detritus of peoples who have left only a wrack behind—the empty chocolate-cartons, torn letters, and obscene hair-combings of the lodgers of the globe" (12/45, 769).

With the April, 1946 issue, Seán O'Faoláin resigned as editor of *The Bell*. In his valedictory editorial he looked back on the first six years of the magazine, findings its strength to be an honest realism and its major limitation to be a lack of "poetic visions of ideal life." For the latter, the times had been inauspicious. The task of *The Bell* had been "less that of cultivating our garden than of clearing away the brambles" (4/46, 1). Looking ahead, he paid homage to an imagined poet who may be "tending in his secret heart a lamp which will, in the end, light far more than we can ever do . . ." And he admonished young writers to begin "close to the nose," finding their way back to the heart, where "the real fight will begin." Even the homeliest pieces in *The Bell* were parables of "the heart's search for the heart. That is all we have brought, in this little magazine, to modern Ireland" (4/46, 4).

It would be unjust to say that after O'Faoláin's resignation the life went out of *The Bell*, but surely its tenor changed. "Seán O'Faoláin *is The Bell*," Vivian Mercier could say in 1945; and with O'Faoláin's departure the magazine lost both the force of his editorial voice and the energy of his obsessions—his passion for Ireland, on the one hand, and for foreign affairs, on the other. The tension between those passions—the one so introverted, the other outward-looking—had given the magazine much of its distinctive character, and under his successor, the novelist and socialist Peadar O'Donnell, that tension largely disappeared. O'Faoláin stayed on as book editor and continued to contribute letters, stories, and essays, including a famous critique of the Hierarchy ("The Dail and the Bishops," 6/51), which stirred no little controversy. But as an editorial force he dropped from sight, and after 1946 his absence is nearly as tangible as his erstwhile presence.

Yet under O'Donnell *The Bell* remained a lively, if somewhat blander, magazine, and in the years after the war, it continued to evolve. If *The Bell* had been, in its early years, an "open window" on Ireland, it became in its maturity an open window on England, Europe, America, and the rest of the postwar world. Rather than write editorials condemning Irish parochialism, O'Donnell set an example by publishing articles on international subjects, most notably Owen Sheehy-Skeffington's regular foreign commentaries, Francis Russell's essays on the Boston Irish, and excerpts from Denis Johnston's exemplary war diaries, which were later collected in *Nine Rivers from Jordan* (1954). During Louis MacNeice's brief tenure as poetry editor (1946-47) the verse substantially improved; and the literary criticism, which had been uneven and impressionistic, grew sturdier with the arrival of Anthony Cronin, who wrote about modern poetry, and Conor Cruise O'Brien, who wrote about Graham Greene, Evelyn Waugh, Francois Mauriac, and other foreign authors. And though the magazine continued to feature such established masters as Lavin and O'Flaherty, it opened its pages to such younger talents as Cronin, Brendan Behan, John Montague, and the irascible Patrick Kavanagh, whose disparagement of Frank O'Connor's poetry in the December, 1947 issue provoked irate responses. Always the abrasive needler, Kavanagh censured O'Connor for keeping his distance from "the earth's healthy reality" and portrayed him as a "purveyor of emotional entertainment." That slur on a Corkman's character sparked an angry letter from O'Faoláin, who accused Kavanagh of demanding his own brand of clay-heavy "realism" from another writer. "All this," O'Faoláin fumed, "is merely Mr. Kavanagh, as usual, roaring contentedly at his own face in the mirror of everything he reads" (1/48, 61).

Despite such evidence of vitality, by 1948 *The Bell* had begun to lose energy. And in April, 1948, three months after the Kavanagh-O'Faoláin exchange, the magazine suspended publication, complaining of financial and spiritual depletion. "I have been of opinion [*sic*]," wrote O'Donnell, "that the original impulse in *The Bell* has exhausted itself, and that if we are to serve any real purpose we must move closer to the problems of the moment—domestic and international" (4/48, 4). In November, 1950, publication resumed, but over the next four years the magazine lost momentum and the will to continue. "Slowly," recalled Hubert Butler, "it began to sag like a balloon from which the air is escaping. Some strong puff of passionate conviction might have inflated it again, but none came." With the December, 1954 issue *The Bell* left the world for good, and what O'Donnell called "a very gallant effort" came to an end.

Had the magazine found its puff of conviction, it might have remained a vibrant force in Irish letters—or become a hoary institution. But by 1954 *The Bell* had lived a full life and had already accomplished much of what its creators had set out to do. As Maurice Harmon has remarked, by 1947 O'Faoláin "could claim with justice that he had helped to clarify intelligible and recognizable elements within the community: liberals, chauvinists, bureaucrats, pietists, professional peasants, native middle classes, the rank and brutal racketeers" (*Seán O'Faoláin*, Wolfhound Press, 51). And though in later years, the magazine's focus shifted to international affairs, *The Bell* continued to stir and shape Irish opinion, as it addressed such issues as sectarianism, Ulster Protestantism, and the political influence of the Catholic Church. To the religious ideologies, as to the mythologies of de Valera and the Gaelic cult, it was both a gall and a potent counterforce. In the view of R.F. Foster (*Modern Ireland: 1600-1972*), it "stands as the record of an alternative culture."

The literary merits of *The Bell* are more difficult to assess. When Vivian Mercier reviewed the magazine in its own pages (May, 1945), he praised its non-fiction and its "realistic" poetry but expressed disappointment with its fiction and especially its editorials, which he found generalized and repetitious. In retrospect, Mercier's verdict seems both wrong-headed and rather bizarre. It underestimates the fiction, which included some of O'Faoláin's, O'Connor's, and O'Flaherty's finest work, and it overestimates the poetry, which included some memorable poems by Hewitt, Kavanagh, Pearse Hutchinson, Sam Harrison, Freda Laughton, MacNeice, and Day-Lewis but suffered, on the whole, from the limitations of its long-standing poetry editor, Geoffrey Taylor, whose tastes ran to the Edwardian-Romantic. Yet Mercier was probably right in seeing the factual, first-person essay as the heartbeat of *The Bell*. And, as the critic noted, many of the earlier essays were written by people who would never write another—people who were describing "the one thing they have really *felt*, really *seen*, in all their lives" (5/45, 160).

To say as much is perhaps to relegate *The Bell* to an inferior literary status, at least when compared with *Horizon*, its leading contemporary. But it is also to recognize its democratic character and its deeply humanistic core. In his editorial farewell O'Faoláin regretted the absence of "noble theories" and "interesting aesthetic ideas" in the pages of his magazine. But elsewhere he remarked that "if *any* ideal does not follow the contours of human nature, it must evaporate . . ." (4/44, 7), and he understood the audience of *The Bell* to be "people who are probably much more sensitive to the Human Comedy, more shrewd about character, more responsive to all its vagaries and subtleties, than many far more cultivated people who live in the kind of society where natural personality has been rolled flat by convention" (1/44, 343–44). That understanding may account for the essential humanity of *The Bell*, which appealed to the heart as well as the intellect but had little time for sentimentality, be it the pastoralism of Eamon de Valera or the "glorification of mere racialism irrespective of talents or brains" (12/43, 186). Such sanity is rare in any era, and for this reader, at least, it remains a tonic and a beacon, whatever the distance or the lapse of years.

1992

Gael and Gall

OF THE HUMAN ATTRIBUTES which could incautiously be labeled Irish, two of the most salient are a genius for language and a native sense of theater. "Our traditions," notes Denis Donoghue in *We Irish*, "are histrionic and oratorical." Donoghue's observation might be challenged, insofar as it demotes the more muted Irish voices or overlooks the obliquity of Irish speech. But the new *Field Day Anthology of Irish Writing*,[1] produced under the auspices of the Field Day Theatre Company of Derry, Northern Ireland, offers ample evidence for Donoghue's claim. Within the four thousand pages of this three-volume set, writers as diverse as Douglas Hyde and George Bernard Shaw, Edmund Spenser and Geoffrey Keating, Jonathan Swift and Aogán Ó Rathaille address questions of linguistic loss and cultural dispossession, British culpability and Irish complicity. Artfully juxta-

---

[1] *The Field Day Anthology of Irish Writing*. General Editor: Seamus Deane. Associate Editors: Andrew Carpenter and Jonathan Williams. Individual sections edited by Proinsias MacCana, Charles Doherty, Terence Dolan, Nicolas Canny, Alan Harrison, Bryan Coleborne, Christopher Murray, Ian Campbell Ross, David Berman, W.J. McCormack, Declan Kiberd, Terence Brown, D.E.S. Maxwell, Seamus Heaney, Luke Gibbons, Augustine Martin, J.C.C. Mays, Tom Paulin, Eoghan Ó hAnluain, and John Wilson Foster. Field Day Publications (Derry, Northern Ireland). Distributed by W.W. Norton and Company. Three volumes. No illustrations. 4,044 pages. $150.00.

posed, those voices argue and debate, creating a lively dialectical drama. And at intervals between the eloquent speakers, the earnest, choric voices of the Field Day editors probe political motives and rank historical significance. When Bryan Coleborne introduces James Ward's pastoral poem "Phoenix Park" (1718) by observing that Ward "chooses to ignore the English mercantilist restrictions on Irish commerce, trade, and shipping," he speaks for the entire Field Day effort. For if the editors' purpose is to "re-present a series of representations concerning the island of Ireland," it is also to construe the meaning of those images and to commit, in the phrase of General Editor Seamus Deane, an "act of definition." At once a theater for orators and a showcase for Irish writers, this massive anthology is also a profound and compelling political statement.

One can hardly envy the editors' task. Not only have they encompassed some 1500 years of "Irish writing," by which they mean works written in English, Latin, Norman French, and Irish-Gaelic by Irish and Anglo-Irish authors. They have also included works *about* Ireland, written by folk as unlikely and un-literary as Charles II and Oliver Cromwell. Not limiting themselves to products of the imagination, they have chosen, in the words of Tom Paulin, to "abandon conventional ideas of the literary and the aesthetic and consider forms of writing that are often dismissed as ephemeral or non-canonical—familiar letters, political speeches, oaths and toasts, sermons, pieces of journalism . . ." (III, 314). Taking a further step, they have also abandoned chronology, so as to show how the interrelationships of "texts" "run athwart the chronological sequence" (Deane, xxii). Works have been arranged under such thematic rubrics as "Language, Class, and Genre," "Cultural Nationalism," and "Challenging the Canon," as well as under such generic categories as "Irish Fiction" and "Anglo-Irish Verse." A handful of authors—Swift, Burke, Goldsmith, Thomas Moore, Maria Edgeworth, Beckett, Joyce, Yeats—have been assigned sections of their own, but most have been distributed, by a kind of editorial bussing, into schools and movements of the editors' choosing. The effect is often illuminating but also disconcerting. What gives coherence to the mass of selections is not the editors' categories, much less the styles of major authors, but the recurrent references to certain pivotal moments—Catholic Emancipation, the Easter Rising, the Year of the French, the Famine—and to certain themes and issues, most prominently those of literary tradition, cultural continuity, national identity, and the vexed question of "translation." Surfacing like whales in their ungovernable sea, those obsessions impart a kind of unity, if not exactly shape, to this sprawling compilation.

"Every writer in the modern world," observes Thomas Kinsella in "The Irish Writer," is the inheritor of a gapped, discontinuous, polyglot tradition" (III, 629). If that is true of European modernists generally, it is more precisely true of the Irish writer, who is the inheritor of multiple literary and cultural traditions, none of them unbroken. When John Banville remarks that "there is an Irish writing, but there isn't an Irish literature," he underscores the fact that for the Irish writer there is no Great Tradition but multiple lineages and strains, including the Irish-Gaelic, the Anglo-Irish, the nationalist, the Northern Protestant, the humanist, and the internationalist—or what Deane has called the tradition of "privacy, insulation, isolation, and exile." There is also the lively tradition of modern Irish drama, embodied in the rivalry of the Gate and Abbey theaters and the efflorescence of amateur productions. And there is the tradition of modern Irish realism, fathered by George Moore and most fully realized in the fiction of Liam O'Flaherty, Frank O'Connor, and Seán O'Faoláin.

In the Field Day anthology, all of these traditions find generous representation, with sometimes surprising results. Within the framework of Bryan Coleburne's selection of Anglo-Irish verse, the poems of Swift lose some of their originality but gain in cultural significance. Under the merciless scrutiny of Shaw, O'Casey, Bulmer Hobson, Conor Cruise O'Brien, and others, the nationalist tradition in general and the Easter Rising in particular appear no less courageous but more mundane and problematical, more compromised by human frailty, than their eulogists would have the world believe. And the liberal-humanist, anti-nationalist strain, articulated in the pages of Frederick Ryan and John Eglinton's *Dana* (1904-5), AE's *Irish Statesman* (1923-309), and Seán O'Faoláin's *The Bell* (1940-54), appears both enduringly potent and doggedly persistent. Opposing the passionate but narrow views of Hyde, Daniel Corkery, Standish O'Grady, and others, *Dana* advocated a literature that would express the "elemental freedom of the human mind, which is really the essential of all independent and therefore national literature" (II, 976). Forty years later, that theme achieves its fullest expression in the "revisionist" editorials of *The Bell*, where O'Faoláin excoriates the nostalgic pieties and stultifying provincialism of the "Gaelic cult."

To find larger continuities in the long span of "Irish writing" is of course a more difficult project. "What the battleaxe of the Dane, the sword of the Norman, the wile of the Saxon were unable to perform," laments Hyde in 1892, "we have accomplished ourselves. We have at last broken the continuity of Irish life . . ." (II, 530). In another context, Thomas Kinsella observes that "silence . . . is the real condition of Irish literature in the nineteenth century . . ." (III, 625). Hyde is speaking of the neglect of Celtic traditions and Kinsella of the loss of the Irish language, but their complaints point to a common reality. As Luke Gibbons reminds us, discontinuity has been "the norm in Irish cultural experience" (III, 566); and the reader who would find the common thread between the earliest dated Irish poem—a verse in praise of St. Colum Cille, c. 597 A.D.—and the most recent by Michael Hartnett or Nuala Ní Dhomhnaill, must exercise imagination as well as industry.

Connections may of course be found in those "dreams of continuity," as Deane describes them, those "heroic lineages" embodied in the archetypes of Cuchulain, Cathleen Ní Houlihan,

Sweeney, and the Sean Van Vocht. But the continuities most evident in the Field Day anthology are seldom so obvious or so concrete. They abide more reclusively in a stance, or attitude toward language—a habit of delectation and playful elaboration which links the anonymous "Western Sayings" of the seventh century with the wordplay of Joyce, Flann O'Brien, and Benedict Kiely. They sparkle in what John Wilson Foster calls the "gift of anecdote" and "idiomatic flair" (III, 939). More broadly, they dwell in a comic, bittersweet view of life—an anarchic, often satiric vision which links the humor of Joyce, O'Brien, Mervyn Wall, Patrick Boyle, and Paul Muldoon to the *Midnight Court* of Bryan Merriman (c. 1749-1805), the anonymous *Parliament of Clan Thomas*, the medieval *Land of Cokaygne*, and other early fruits of the Irish comic imagination. Since the late seventeenth century, a more baneful continuity may be found in the myths of Green and Orange, the nationalist and loyalist versions of Irish history, astutely analyzed in T.W. Moody's *Hermathena* (1977). Whether it be the Orange order portraying itself as the opponent of European dictatorship, or the Provisional IRA defining itself as the chief architect of Irish destiny, those myths form a living link between the battles of Kinsale, Aughrim, and the Boyne and the intractable violence of the present day.

The myths of Irish nationalism have been especially tenacious, and in the view of Conor Cruise O'Brien and other revisionist critics, those myths have been inseparable from the force and continuity of Irish Catholicism. In *Passion and Cunning* (1988), O'Brien argues that "the main theme of Irish history, for nearly three centuries now, has been the recovery of the Irish Catholics: the Catholics getting their own back, in more senses than one" (III, 595). And in the Fenian movement O'Brien sees "the uncontaminated continuity of Irish Catholic feeling," by which he means "root-and-branch hostility to the British Crown and all it [stands] for" (III, 597). However, he also traces the tension between the Fenians and the bishops, the proponents of violent insurrection and the defenders of constitutional nationalism. That tension reaches its height in Father Francis Shaw's important article, "The Canon of Irish History—A Challenge" (1972), where Shaw passionately condemns Padraic Pearse's doctrine of blood-sacrifice and his appropriation of religious imagery for political ends. Less dramatically, revisionist historians like Moody, Seán O'Faoláin, and Roy Foster have endeavored to separate the strands of Irish Republicanism from those of Irish Catholicism and to dispel, in Foster's phrase, "the old Corkery idea that Catholic and Gaelic were morally congruent with 'Irish'" (III, 585). Complementing the work of the historians and critics, modern Catholic novelists and poets, most notably O'Faoláin, O'Connor, Patrick Kavanagh, Mary Lavin, and Edna O'Brien, have affirmed the centrality of the Church in matters cultural and spiritual, while questioning its moral and political authority and its exclusive claim on Irish national identity.

To speak of Irish identity is of course to join a debate that has preoccupied Irish minds for nearly a century. When Stanislaus Joyce observes that "nothing is stable in the country; nothing is stable in the minds of the people" (III, 670), he overstates his case, but where national identity is concerned, he exaggerates only slightly. For in Ireland, identity has been more than a nagging enigma. It has been a dynamic configuration—a concoction of native self-image and colonial stereotype, harsh rural experience and the fictions of a ruling elite. Its literary progeny include Captain O'Blunder and the dark-eyed Gael, the stage-Irish buffoon and the moody Celt. Its popular archetype, exploded by Shaw in *John Bull's Other Island* (1904), is that of the wild, irrational Irish dreamer, short on logic but long on drink and idle speculation. One of the achievements of the Field Day project is to chronicle the long lineage of such stereotypes and to demonstrate the depth of their penetration into the national psyche. Whether the aggressor has been the Norman topographer Giraldus Cambrensis (c. 1146-1223), who could find nothing commendable in the "wild and inhospitable" Irish but their musicianship, or the colonial apologist Edmund Spenser, who viewed the natives as tractable barbarians, it has been the task of cultural historians like Geoffrey Keating (c. 1580-1650) to refute such slurs and to forge a plausible national identity. In modern Ireland, as Liam de Paor persuasively argues, that task has devolved to the State; and at present, "it is not a sense of identity which sustains the State but the State. . . which sustains a sense of national identity" (III, 664). And as Deane demonstrates in his selection of memoirs and auto-biographies, the pressure of colonial and post-colonial versions of identity has been felt at the personal as well as the public level. In the memoirs of Austin Clarke, Elizabeth Bowen, Louis MacNeice, Ernie O'Malley, Synge, and many others, Deane perceives a struggle "to identify the other force, the hostile or liberating ener-gy, which made the self come into consciousness. . ." And in a "colonial or neo-colonial country like Ireland, the forms of 'oth-erness' available are multiple and blatant. . ." (III, 380). Resisting or absorbing the Other's oppressive definitions, the Irish writer fashions or tries to fashion both a national and a personal identi-ty. As Declan Kiberd reminds us, the exiled, disaffected Shaw "sprang from his own conception of himself, as 'G.B.S.', a pure self-creation" (II, 421).

But can a genuine identity be fashioned in the absence of the Irish language? Can a broken tradition be mended without first recovering its ancient tongue? Since the era of the Literary Revival those questions have been heatedly debated, and in the pages of the Field Day anthology the debate continues, modified and enhanced by international and post-nationalist perspectives. "The death of a language," laments Kinsella, "it is a calamity" (III, 626). And like Kinsella's own *Poems of the Dispossessed* (1981) and his revision of *The Oxford Book of Irish Verse* (1986) the Field Day anthology is an act of repossession, in which the presentation of original Irish texts and the printing of modern translations play equally important parts. For Deane and the Field

Day editors, the act of translation is "profoundly political." It is both an act of nationalistic self-assertion and a gesture toward cultural reconciliation. "It is not necessarily true," Deane argues, "that something always gets lost in translation. It is necessarily true that translation is founded on the idea of loss and recuperation; it might be understood as an action that takes place in the interval between these alternatives" (I, xxv). For the philosopher Richard Kearney, "there is no unitary master narrative of Irish cultural history, but a plurality of transitions between different perspectives" (III, 633). Faithful or faltering, the act of translation is the central agent of those transitions.

"Translation," figuratively considered, is also a central component of the Field Day enterprise, influencing the editors' selections and allotments of space. It is no accident that Deane grants extensive space to Thomas Moore, whose *Irish Melodies* (1808-34) translated "something wild and savage into something regulated and polished" (I, 1055), and even more to the "London exiles" Shaw and Wilde, whose plays reflect their divided loyalties and form a bridge between the divided cultures. Likewise the fifty-page selection of Burke's pro-Catholic writings, which express both his loyalty to British hierarchies and his abhorrence of British oppression. But if the Field Day project may be said to have an ur-text or thematic center of gravity, it is Brian Friel's play *Translations* (1980), which is reprinted in its entirety in the third volume and brings the anthology to its thematic climax.

Set in the fictive parish of Ballybeg in nineteenth-century Donegal, *Translations* pits a fragmented native populace against a contingent of British military surveyors, who have been assigned the task of re-mapping the parish and Anglicizing Gaelic place-names. When a British soldier and a local woman fall in love, tragic violence ensues. In this parable of cultural collision and absorption, Richard Kearney sees both a "translation of labor" and a "translation of love," while Edna Longley finds only nostalgia and a refurbishing of "an old myth." At issue is the question of whether the act of translation, supported or resisted by a fractured people, disrupts or preserves the continuity of Irish traditions and the integrity of Gaelic culture.

To probe such questions is the express purpose of the Field Day editors, and they have acquitted themselves admirably, though not without cost to other purposes and values. Edna Longley has wittily characterized the Field Day outlook as an uneasy mixture of Derry and Derrida; and though the editors' prose steers clear of fashionable obfuscation, their outlook bears the influence of fashionable ideologies. In one sweeping sentence Deane dismisses the "aesthetic ideology" as a "political force which pretends not to be so" (I, xxvi). And with rare exceptions, his anthology reflects a subordination of aesthetic to political values. In volume II Augustine Martin cites limitation of space as the reason for excluding Seumas O'Kelly's beautiful, serio-comic story, "The Weaver's Grave." But that same volume includes some one hundred and fifty pages of "Political Writings and Speeches," many of them lengthy and tedious. In volume III John Wilson Foster justly regrets that his selection of contemporary Irish fiction cannot "spare room" for Bryan MacMahon and Molly Keane. But elsewhere in that volume more than two hundred pages are spared for partisan political oratory. No one need quarrel with the inclusion of Padraic Pearse's moving graveside eulogy for O'Donovan Rossa—or care whether it is "literature" or not. But Deane's inclusion of Pearse's rather bad poem "The Wayfarer," reputed to have been written on the eve of his execution, can be justified only be reference to its political occasion. When Deane chooses to include Lionel Johnson's "Ninety-Eight" and "Parnell" after admitting that "Johnson's poems on Irish subjects are very far from his best" (II, 720), the purpose and the bias of the Field Day project come sharply into focus.

And is there not, in the editors' sober efforts to order and rationalize "Irish writing," a strange inharmony of form and content? At more than one point in the anthology, the concerted effort to commit an "act of definition" is curiously at odds with the exuberant, grotesque, and anarchic tendencies of Irish writing. And in its encounters with the likes of O'Connor, O'Faoláin, Edna O'Brien, and Mary Lavin, the editors' political agenda seems more than a little discordant with the lyrical, tolerant, and forgiving sensibilities of the greatest Irish writers. Deane is pleased to have demonstrated the "endless fecundity" (I, xxvi) of Irish writing, as well he might be. But in its schematic presentation of an overflowing abundance, his anthology succeeds almost in spite of itself.

Although the editors never say so—and might not care to admit it—their anthology is also a testament to the ubiquity and force of Irish eloquence, whether the speaker be Shaw or Daniel O'Connell, Yeats or Joyce, John Montague or Seamus Heaney. Beckett once remarked that if "you really get down to the disaster, the slightest eloquence becomes unbearable" (III, 233); and for Declan Kiberd, the eloquence of the Abbey plays is often "a kind of consolation for poverty" (III, 1313). Kiberd notes Yeats's "fatal propensity for eloquence," and he dismisses praise for "Irish eloquence" as a patronizing, Anglo-American attitude (III, 639). If that be true, however, Kiberd may have to include Joyce himself among the culpable perpetrators. For it was Joyce who observed that

> in spite of everything, Ireland remains the brain of the United Kingdom. The English, judiciously practical and ponderous, furnish the overstuffed stomach of humanity with a perfect gadget—the water closet. The Irish, condemned to express themselves in a language not their own, have stamped on it the mark of their genius and compete for glory with the civilized nations.

To that achievement, as to "Irish writing" generally, the Field Day anthology is a momentous and monumental tribute.

1992

After the Coronachs[1]

In one of his most poignant elegies, Derek Mahon pays a visit to Derry City in Northern Ireland. The year is 1979—eleven years after the first protests and the elevation of that provincial town to the world stage. With a mixture of muted astonishment and meditative calm, Mahon surveys the "shining roofs and murmuring schools," the rubble and bomb-holes:

> Hard to believe this tranquil place,
> Its desolation almost peace,
> Was recently a boom-town wild
> With expectation, each unscheduled
> Incident a measurable
> Tremor on the Richter Scale
> Of world events, each vibrant scene
> Translated to the drizzling screen.

---

[1] This essay makes reference to the following books: Derek Mahon, *The Hunt By Night* (Wake Forest University Press, 1982); Denis Donoghue, *We Irish* (Knopf, 1986); Seamus Heaney, *Place and Displacement* (Dove Cottage, 1985); Medbh McGuckian, *The Flower Master* (Oxford University Press, 1982) and *Venus and the Rain* (Oxford, 1984); Tom Paulin, *A State of Justice* (Faber and Faber, 1977), *The Strange Museum* (Faber, 1980), *Liberty Tree* (Faber, 1983), and *Ireland and the English Crisis* (Newcastle: Bloodaxe Books, 1984); Ciarán Carson, *The New Estate* (Wake Forest, 1976), and *The Irish for No* (Wake Forest, 1987); Benedict Kiely, *Proxopera* (Gollancz, 1977) and *Nothing Happens in Carmincross* (Godine, 1985); Paul Muldoon, *Mules and Early Poems* (Wake Forest, 1985) and *Meeting the British* (Wake Forest, 1987); and Edna Longley, *Poetry in the Wars* (Bloodaxe, 1986).

Adopting a long historical perspective, wherein the centuries take "two steps forward, one step back," Mahon looks with detachment on a "fitful revolution," whose hopes have swelled and dwindled:

> What of the change envisioned here,
> The quantum leap from fear to fire?
> Smoke from a thousand chimneys strains
> One way beneath the returning rains
> That shroud the bomb-sites, while the fog
> Of time receives the ideologue.
> A Russian freighter bound for home
> Mourns to the city in its gloom.
>
> ("Derry Morning" in *The Hunt by Night*)

Mahon's closing couplet strikes a familiar chord. It is the tonality of tragic resignation, which has prevailed in Irish poetry since the late seventeenth century, uniting the late-bardic dirges of Daibhi Ó Bruadair and Aogán Ó Rathaille with the more recent laments of Thomas Kinsella and John Montague. In Mahon's poem, as in those of his forbears, public and private themes commingle, and the sorrows of an exile are mirrored in Ireland's melancholy history.

The elegiac note can also be heard in the younger poets or Northern Ireland, but even the casual observer will notice that something has changed. Elegy is giving way to disgust, or despair, or a dark irreverence. Traditional pieties are being undermined or set aside. Recently Seamus Heaney remarked that Paul Muldoon, the leading younger poet of the North, has been "changing the rules by which the game is played"; but the same is true, in varying degrees, of Muldoon's talented and often sardonic contemporaries, most notably Tom Paulin, Medbh McGuckian, and Ciarán Carson. Unlike the writers of Heaney's generation, whose careers were invaded by the Troubles, these poets have come of age in an atmosphere of bombings and sectarian atrocities. They have also grown up in a critical spotlight, subjected, on the one side, to pressure for political engagement, and on the other, to the suspicion that in dealing with the Troubles they are exploiting a painful national crisis. Wary and weary of those pressures, they have produced a body of writing marked by a keen sense of irony and a guarded sense of privacy, by extremes of engagement and disengagement, by parabolic and elliptical forms, and by ventures into a black absurdist humor reminiscent of Eastern Europe. "Forget the corncrake's elegy," Ciarán Carson declares, as he casts a cold eye on a Belfast housing estate. In rhetoric and feeling that is a far cry from John Montague's laments for his "broken province," or Heaney's reverential invocations of Irish place-names.

The younger poets have not turned their backs on Irish problems or abandoned the longings of an earlier generation. It would be fairer to say that they have taken a more knowing, less patient, and often less insular attitude toward the dilemmas that have vexed Irish writers for nearly a century. For Muldoon's generation, as for Heaney's and Kavanagh's and Synge's, there is the gnawing question of identity, national and personal—a problem of peculiar intensity in the North of Ireland, where the claims of Unionists vie with those of Irish nationalists. There is the question of allegiance, literary and political, in a country with two languages and two poetic traditions: the ancient, fragmented Irish-Gaelic, on the one hand, and the imposed but established Anglo-Irish, on the other. There is, as always, the enigma of Irish history, made stranger by the fact that, as Denis Donoghue remarks in *We Irish* (1986), children are now being told, "some for the first time, that Irish history is plural rather than singular, that our country is the result of mixed parentage, that Catholics and Protestants equally share the fate of being Irish." And there is the nagging question of political commitment, with voices as strong as Edna Longley's urging the separation of poetry from politics, and others, such as Tom Paulin's, urging partisan engagement. At odds with both extremes, Muldoon and others have sought a middle ground: a stance which Heaney, in *Place and Displacement* (1985) has defined as "neither deliberately provocative nor culpably detached." They have also sought transcendence, a graceful exit from public quarrels and regional concerns, whether through private meditations on lovers, friends and family, or through analogies with earlier periods, or through emblems of Irish unity and concord. Among the more visionary, there has been talk of a Fifth Province—a non-geographical, apolitical center where bigotry has no place.

Of those poets who have turned inward, finding sustenance not in public debate but in the rigors of introspection, Medbh McGuckian is at once the most fluent and the most hermetic. "A woman ripens best underground," she insists, taking as her subjects the reclusive atmospheres of gardens and domestic interiors, the essences of flowers, trees, fabrics, and foodstuffs, the recesses of intimate relationships. Born in 1950 and educated at a convent school, McGuckian has been described by Anne Stevenson as a "contemporary, Irish Emily Dickinson," and the description is apt, insofar as it connotes a fierce sense of privacy and an alertness to ferment beneath external composure. "My heart, alas, / Is not the calmest of places," McGuckian reminds herself; and in a poem addressed to her grandmother she teases out feelings of helplessness and blocked affection:

> I would revive you with a swallow's nest:
> For as long a time as I could hold my breath
> I would feel your pulse like tangled weeds
> Separate into pearls. The heart should rule
> The summer, ringing like a sickle over
> The need to make life hard. I would
> Sedate your eyes with rippleseed, those
> Hollow points that close as if
> Your eyelids had been severed to
> Deny you sleep, imagine you a dawn.
>
> ("To My Grandmother")

Here, as often in McGuckian's poems, a strong sense of line competes with the pressure of strong enjambment ("those / Hollow points that close . . ."), and a dense, riddling idiom, suggestive of emotional congestion, is played off against the clarity of repeated assertions ("I would revive you . . ."; "I would / Sedate your eyes . . ."). Beneath these formal devices lies an inner drama, a private conflict of circumstance and will. Faced with her grandmother's pain and withdrawal, the speaker longs to intervene. She would be the agent of healing and renewal. Instead, she encounters the depth of her grandmother's suffering and the limits of her own restorative powers. Youthful or no, she can hold her breath for only so long.

McGuckian has published two full-length collections, *The Flower Master* (1982) and *Venus and the Rain* (1984), and between them lies more continuity than change, more consistency than development. Through both volumes she maintains the solitude and inner freedom of one who owes

> no older debt
> Than to the obligatory palette of the rain,
> That brought the soil back into tension on my slope,
> And the sea in, making me an island once again.
>
> ("Dovecote")

In her more recent poems, McGuckian has pondered the mysteries of personal relationships. The mother of two children, she has explored the maternal bond, discovering distance and agitation rather than a comforting stability:

> Child in the centre of the dark parquet,
> Sleepy, glassed-in child, my fair copy,
> While you were sailing your boat in the bay,
> I saw you pass along the terrace twice,
> Flying in the same direction as the epidemic
> Of leaves in the hall.
>
> ("Confinement")

And in her poems on love and marriage, she has chastened her romantic yearnings with a stern Northern realism:

> To the nightingale it made no difference
> Of course, that you tossed about an hour,
> Two hours, till what was left of your future
> Began: nor to the moon that nearly rotted,
> Like the twenty-first century growing
> Its grass through me. But became in the end,
> While you were still asleep, a morning
> Where I saw our neighbors' mirabelle,
> Bent over our hedge, and its trespassing
> Fruit, unacknowledged as our own.
>
> ("To the Nightingale")

In these supple lines, a romantic imagination yields to a classical sense of human limitation. Both the title phrase and its romantic emblem merge with a reminder of the natural world's indifference, and a cherished recollection gives way to a sobering vision of the future. Beyond her verbal agilities, McGuckian's salient strength lies in her ability to articulate ambiguities of this kind. It is a gift she shares with her older countrywoman, Mary Lavin, who once defined the short story as the art of looking more closely than normal into the human heart.

In one of her rare outward looks, McGuckian recalls her experience at Ireland's military checkpoints, where British soldiers patrol the border between the Republic and Northern Ireland:

> At the checkpoints it occurs to me,
> My measurements at nine,
> My secret box stuffed with peacock's feathers.
>
> ("Admiring the Furs")

If these lines assert the supremacy of personal memory over political realities, of personal concerns over political issues, quite the opposite occurs in the poems of Tom Paulin, for whom a checkpoint would be an occasion for political reflection. More

than any other Irish poet of his generation, Paulin has confront-
ed the "steel polities" of Ulster and the impersonal forces of his-
tory, bringing his lyric gifts to a kind of public service. In his best
poems he has achieved a fusion of hard objectivity and lyric
intensity.

Paulin was born in Leeds, England in 1949, but grew up in
Belfast. His early poems, collected in *A State of Justice* (1977),
savor the obduracy of things—the hardness of urban brick and
northern granite, the "gantries, mills and steeples" of Belfast and
the "waste, silent valleys" of Co. Antrim. Like Louis MacNeice,
whose spirit lingers over *A State of Justice*, Paulin is ambivalent
toward his native ground, relishing its austerities while decrying
its desolation:

> The grey hills of that country fall away
> > Like folds of skin. There are some mountains somewhere
> And public parks with metal fountains.
>
> > > ("Cadaver Politic")

Brooding on that bleak landscape, Paulin recalls that under the
cover of those hills, "clans are at their manoeuvres." And in his
more recent poems, collected in *The Strange Museum* (1980) and
Liberty Tree (1983) he inspects the psychic damage wreaked by
sectarian conflict and military occupation. In "Surveillances," a
helicopter circles above the terraced houses, leaving Paulin with a
sense of unreality, as if "[a]ll this [were] happening / Under-
water." In "Martello," as he surveys the vestiges of British occu-
pation, he feels a vague sense of complicity:

> There is a dead vigilance along this coast,
> a presence that bruises like the word *British*.
> You can catch the atmosphere of neglected garrisons,
> and the rusted aftertaste of bully beef
> in the dashed surprise of a cement watchtower
>
> ruined on a slope of ragweed and bullocks grazing.
> In the dovegrey Victorian hotel

a spooly sways at the bar and says,
"We're nearly a nation now, before the year's out
they'll maybe write Emmet's epitaph."

Can you *describe* history I'd like to know?
Isn't it a fiction that pretends to be fact
like *A Journal of the Plague Year?*
And the answer that snaps back at me
is a winter's afternoon in Dungannon,
the gothic barracks where the policemen
were signing out their weapons in a stained register,
a thick turbid light and that brisk smell of fear
as I described the accident and felt guilty—
guilty for no reason, or cause, I could think of.

Paul grew up in a strict Scots Presbyterian family, but before he
had left for the university he had joined a Trotskyite organization
and had rejected Ulster Calvinism in favor of Marxist dialectic. "I
pretty well despise official Protestant culture," he says flatly,
though he has remained fascinated with a people "who can simul-
taneously wave the Union Jack and yet hate the English, as many
Protestants do." In "Martello," Paulin alludes on the one hand to
an Irish patriot's speech from the dock, and on the other to an
Englishman's fictive account of the London plague. It was Robert
Emmet (1778-1803), the condemned rebel, who asked that no man
write his epitaph until his century had taken its place among the
nations of the world—a nationalist text that Paulin's barfly
remembers. And it was Defoe who blurred the line between his-
tory and fiction, creating an early example of the historical novel.
By juxtaposing these disparate texts with the ruins of British
occupation, with the menacing presence of the Protestant con-
stabulary in Dungannon, and with his own sense of unresolved
guilt, Paulin broods on the ironies of history, the uncertainties of
historical description, and the complicity of his ancestors in colo-
nial oppression.

Not all of Paulin's meditations are so grim. "Like lead dropping in a shot-tower," goes one of his epigrams, "Clio's voice has no feeling"; and if he remains committed, in the bulk of his work, to a precise historicism, he also remains alert to moments of transcendence. Leaving Inishkeel Parish Church, he looks out on "an enormous sight of the sea, / A silent water beyond society." Elsewhere, he positions himself in "the long lulled pause / before history happens," or envisions the "stillness / Of a pure landscape," or invents a southern "garden of self-delight," where "fine and gracious beings . . . pass me by and sing / lightly to each other." Against a backdrop of historical determinism, he celebrates moments of timeless intimacy:

> Those luminous privacies
> On a bleached coast
> Are fierce and authentic,
> And some of us believe in them.
> They are the polities of love.
>
> ("Purity")

Yet in the same poem he views a "crowded troopship / Moving down the blue lough / On a summer's morning, / Its anal colours / Almost fresh in the sun."

Paulin's most original poems temper his lyric music with a laconic factuality. They propound what the poet has called a "factual idealism." At his most visionary, he also imagines a united Ireland, a federation of languages and cultures. In "A New Look at the Language Question" (in *Ireland and the English Crisis*, 1984) Paulin examines the efforts of Swift, Johnson, Fowler, James Murray and others to establish a standard English language. In their place he proposes, for Ireland, a "federal concept of Irish-English," a "new public language" braided from the strands of Irish, Ulster Scots, and Irish English. Paulin's own recent poems toy with a synthesis of that kind, interweaving Irish, Ulster dialect, and standard English idiom:

Here's a wet sheugh
smells like a used sheath,
and here's frogspawn
and a car battery

under a screggy hawthorn.

("S/he")

Edna Longley has denounced such efforts as patronizing, and for
the most part they create darkness rather than light, obscurity
rather than a civil tongue. More compelling, if a little short of
convincing, is Paulin's vision of national unity, embodied in the
emblem of the juniper:

Consider
the gothic zigzags
and brisk formations
that square to meet
the green tide rising
through Mayo and Antrim,

now dream
of that sweet
equal republic
where the juniper
talks to the oak,
the thistle,
the bandaged elm,
and the jolly jolly chestnut.

("The Book of Juniper")

These lean lines do not so much depart from as advance Paulin's
hard-edged realism. Their lyric clarity girds their purity of vision.

But can such moments counterbalance the weight of historical
memory? Have their remedies any efficacy? As one might expect,
visions of unity are rare in the work of Paulin and his contempo-

raries, where one is more likely to encounter a nervous tone and an imagery of demolition and centrifugal dispersal. For all her self-possession, Medbh McGuckian writes, in one poem, of a "waterfall / Unstitching itself down the front stairs," and in another, of a "deadly freckled junkyard." And in the recent, free-wheeling poems of Ciarán Carson we enter a world in nearly total disarray—an urban landscape littered with rubble and broken glass, where the obliteration of landmarks has left the inhabitants of Belfast in a state of perpetual dislocation:

The linen backing is falling apart—the Falls Road hangs by a thread.
When someone asks me where I live, I remember where I used to
    live.
Someone asks me for directions, and I think again, I turn into
A side-street to try to throw off my shadow, and history is changed.

                          ("Turn Again")

    Born in 1948, Carson grew up in Catholic Belfast. His first language was Irish, and his first collection of poems, *The New Estate* (1976), published when the poet was only twenty-eight, includes his deft translations from his native language:

    Behind the hedged lines where I write,
    The blackbird sings a dawn
    Of parchment held to the light.

                 ("The Scribe in the Woods")

This is one of Carson's many homages to Irish legend, craft, and tradition. In one memorable poem he celebrates the communal effort of bell-casting, the transformation of "the glittering ore / of chalices and plates" into a "sounding-bow of bronze / ringing out unchanging noons." In another he likens the solitary labors and "endless repetitions" of a weaver to

        the loneliness
      of human passion,

    ◂◂

the pain that must
in the end give meaning
to the grass and trees
that blur outside the door.

("Interior with Weaver")

Although they explore personal anguish, these early poems look away from political unrest. "You like dilapidation," Carson tells his sister, in a poem about moving into a rundown house; and elsewhere, as he contemplates a snow-covered junkyard, he finds both beauty and a "detritus of lights." But his main concern is with the solidities of care and craft, even when speaking of bombs:

Is it just like picking a lock
with the slow deliberation of a funeral,
hesitating through a darkened nave
until you find the answer?

Listening to the malevolent tick
of its heart, can you read
the message of the threaded veins
like print, its body's chart?"

("The Bomb Disposal")

Here it is not the menace of the bomb that engages Carson's attention, so much as the mystery of its mechanism and the meticulous skill of those sent to disarm it.

Perhaps only a writer steeped in Irish traditions could have written the disturbing poems of Carson's second collection, *The Irish for No* (1987), published after an eleven-year silence. Rather than honor Irish continuities, they evoke the anguish and incipient chaos of a troubled province, where continuity has all but vanished. It is tempting to say that in these poems Carson has found his authentic voice, but it would be truer to say that he has found the crackling, despairing, self-mocking voice of contemporary Belfast. In their long colloquial lines, their catalogs of debris and ephemeral brand names, they evoke a city's weariness and instability, its yearning for solidity and wholeness. The dominant metaphor is that of a map, expressive both of Carson's longing for order and of his awareness that the city of Belfast, like a map of a city, is subject at any time to arbitrary revision. Where there was once continuity, there is now a profusion of doubts:

> Suddenly as the riot squad moved in, it was raining
>   exclamation marks,
> Nuts, bolts, nails, car-keys. A fount of broken type. And the
>   explosion
> Itself—an asterisk on the map . . .
>
>   What is
> My name? Where am I coming from? Where am I going? A
>   fusillade of question marks.
>
>   ("Belfast Confetti")

In response to chaos and emptiness, to such sights as a blown-up marketplace, "[e]verything unstitched, unraveled—mouldy fabric,/ Rusted heaps of nuts and bolts...obliterated streets," Carson elects, more often than not, to laugh rather than cry. Hollow or hearty, his sardonic laughter echoes through his poems, enlivening such stories as that of Horse Boyle, a second world war veteran haunted by memories of bombing Dresden, who lives in a decrepit trailer, surrounded by "baroque pyramids of empty baked bean tins." In darker moods, as in a poem about British soldiers on patrol, Carson's comedy turns to satire:

> The duck patrol is waddling down the odd-numbers side of Raglan
>   Street,
> The bass-ackwards private at the rear trying not to think of a third
>   eye
> Being drilled in the back of his head. . . .

* * *

Number one. Ormond Street. *Two ducks in front of a duck and two ducks*
Behind a duck, how many ducks? Five? *No. Three.* This is not the end.

("Army")

No laughing matter? For better or worse, laughter seems a protective, necessary response—or an assertion of inner freedom. In his title poem, Carson jumbles a sectarian war cry with an advertising slogan, creating a bizarre linguistic stew:

> It was time to turn into the dog's-leg short-cut from Chlorine
> Gardens
> Into Cloreen Park, where you might see an *Ulster Says No*
> scrawled on the side
> Of the power-block—which immediately reminds me of the
> Eglantine Inn
> Just on the corner: on the missing *h* of Cloreen, you might say.
> We were debating,
> Bacchus and the pards and me, how to render *The Ulster Bank—*
> *the Bank*
> *That Likes to Say Yes* into Irish, and whether eglantine was alien
> to Ireland.

("The Irish for No")

A nod and a wink to Keats? A comment on the betrayal of language? Underlying this enigmatic joke is the political status of the Irish language in the North of Ireland, its role as a nationalist bonding-agent and its banishment by the Protestant hegemony. To deepen the irony, there is also the fact that Irish-Gaelic contains no specific words for *yes* and *no*.

Ciarán Carson is not alone in finding black humor in Ulster's tragedy. A similar laughter erupts in the fiction of Benedict Kiely, whose recent novels, *Proxopera* (1977) and *Nothing Happens in Carmincross* (1985), make bitter comedy of senseless atrocities. Laughter also ripples through the poems of Paul Muldoon, thirty years Kiely's junior, though its objects are often more ambiguous, its origins more obscure.

At thirty-seven, Muldoon is the best-known Irish poet of his generation, with a substantial reputation in Ireland, England, and the United States. Although he has lived most of his adult life in Belfast, moving only recently to New York, Muldoon grew up in rural Co. Armagh, and his earliest poems, collected in *New Weather* (1973), combine an imagery of meadows and woods with a high degree of obliquity, urbanity, and intellectual sophistication. In his subsequent collections he has probed the tensions of Belfast, but he has seldom done so in any literal—much less confessional—way. "As it occurs in the poems," Muldoon has explained, "my family is from the earliest invented, invented brothers and sisters and mothers and fathers."[2] His forte has been the parable, or parabolic anecdote, his vehicle the dramatic persona, whether it take the form of a poet having lunch with Pancho Villa, or a servant girl recounting a mysterious incident at a Big House, or the voices of Auden, MacNeice, and Benjamin Britten discoursing on art and literature.

The job of the writer, Muldoon believes, is "so far as any of us can . . . to be a free agent, within the state of oneself, or roaming through the different states of oneself." To preserve that freedom Muldoon has steered clear of political parties, and in the rhetoric of his poems he has often assumed the roles of outsider, mediator, or curious observer. In the title poem of his second collection (1985) he looks with wry detachment on a beast that bridges divisions:

> Should they not have the best of both worlds?
>
> Her feet of clay gave the lie
> To the star burned in our mare's brow.
> Would Parsons' jackass not rest more assured
> That cross wrenched from his shoulders?

---

[2]Kevin Barry, "Q. & A.: Paul Muldoon," *The Irish Literary Supplement* 6, No. 2 (Fall 1987): 37.

We had loosed them into one field.
I watched Sam Parsons and my quick father
Tense for the punch below their belts,
For what was neither one thing or the other.

("Mules")

Muldoon has explained that he wrote these lines after seeing a
newsreel image of mules being dropped by parachute. That
bizarre image is paralleled in the condition of the newborn foal,
its suspension between the celestial and terrestrial worlds, the star
on the brow and the feet of clay, the holy and the homely.
Muldoon's elegant locutions and fluid assonantal music celebrate
both the mystery of the mule's birth and its transcendence of
conventional categories. Like the free agent roaming through
states of the self, the foal is neither one thing or the other.

Muldoon's play of the mind often takes the forms of parody
and comic incongruity. In *Poetry in the Wars* (1986) Edna Longley
has compared Muldoon to a double agent, or secret agent, or
escaped prisoner of war, but the tone of those terms is a little too
political. Muldoon might best be described as an intellectual
demolitionist—the enemy of sectarian pieties, social pretensions,
and literary clichés. Under his scrutiny virtually everything is ripe
for deflation, be it an Anglican bishop, an American literary
celebrity, or the Bard of Sligo's sacred texts.

Muldoon's agility is conspicuous in "7, Middagh Street," the
most ambitious poem in *Meeting the British* (1987). Set in the
Brooklyn Heights home of George Davis, the poem presents the
monologues of seven luminaries of the forties who lived or visit-
ed there. Among them is Louis MacNeice, who explains that his
father, an Anglican bishop, "preached 'Forget the past' / and
episcopized / into the wind . . ." "[N]o bishop," he goes on to say,
"could ever quite contemplate / a life merely nasty, British, and
short." Elsewhere, glancing over her shoulder at Yeats, Gypsy
Rose Lee explains that "there's more enterprise in walking not
quite / naked," and W.H. Auden, reflecting on the efficacy of
poetry, remembers Yeats's "The Man and the Echo":

And were Yeats living at this hour
it should be in some ruined tower

not malachited Ballylee
where he paid out to those below

one gilt-edged scroll from his pencil
as though he were part-Rapunzel

and partly Delphic oracle.
As for his crass, rhetorical

posturing, 'Did that play of mine
send out certain men (*certain* men?)

the English shot. . . ?'
the answer is 'Certainly not'.

If Yeats had saved his pencil-lead
would certain men have stayed in bed?

For history's a twisted root
with art its small, translucent fruit

and never the other way round.
The roots by which we were once bound

are severed here, in any case,
and we are all now dispossessed;

To American readers nurtured on Yeats and accustomed to think-
ing of the Irish poet's place as privileged and influential, these
neat couplets may be jarring. They turn Auden's famous dictum,
("poetry makes nothing happen") into a rebuke, and they suggest
that dispossession is a modern, rather than a peculiarly Irish, con-
dition. Since the time of George Moore, literary Dublin has
poked fun at Yeats's pretensions, but is there not something new
in Muldoon's lightness of touch, his strong autonomous voice,
and his international perspective?

In Muldoon's ironic humor, as in Ciarán Carson's visions of

chaos, Tom Paulin's dreams of unity, and Medbh McGuckian's inward-spiralling lines, one senses a hunger to have done with heroic postures and polemics and to be free of the familiar Irish constraints. For all their eloquence, modern Irish writers have been hampered by political allegiances, inherited identities, and self-limiting concepts of the poet as elegist and bard. They have been wedded to the backward look and the elegiac mode. If they now seem inclined to make a bride of irony, and to assert the freedom of the *eiron*, that may be a salutary change.

1988

Angel in Clay

TWENTY YEARS after his death, Patrick Kavanagh has emerged as the dominant influence in contemporary Irish poetry. During his lifetime Kavanagh made his presence felt, both as the author of *The Great Hunger* (1942) and as an outspoken critic, who blasted his fellow writers and left bruised egos wherever he turned. Kavanagh's posthumous presence is no less potent, though it has grown less abrasive. In rural County Monaghan, where Kavanagh grew up, he is remembered as a dreamer and a desultory farmer. In literary Dublin, where he scratched out a living as a film reviewer, columnist, and co-publisher of the ill-fated *Kavanagh's Weekly*, he is remembered as the gentle elegist of Baggot Street, the loser in a celebrated libel suit, the strident habitué of the Palace Bar. And in the minds of younger Irish poets, Kavanagh looms large as the Catholic, demotic alternative to the mandarin, Anglo-Irish bard of Sligo. Seamus Heaney acknowledges as much in his "Station Island" sequence, where Heaney's pilgrim-persona, doing penance at Lough Derg, meets up with the "slack-shouldered," "clear-eyed" shade of the older poet. "Sure I might have known," says Kavanagh to Heaney, "you'd be after me / sooner or later. Forty-two years on / and you've got no farther!" As if to mock Heaney's spiritual ambitions, Kavanagh adds: "In my own day / the odd one came here on the hunt for women."

Heaney's sketch is caricature, but it also approximates the

truth. For Patrick Kavanagh was neither the pure cynic, nor the incurable idealist, nor that more familiar figure, the youthful romantic turned sardonic elder. From first to last he remained the doubting pilgrim, the "half-faithed ploughman" of his early verse. For better or worse, saint and sinner share crowded quarters in Kavanagh's *Complete Poems*,[1] which gathers more than two hundred and fifty poems on subjects as diverse as Kavanagh's Monaghan childhood, the Easter Rising, Ulster virtue, Dublin women, film stars, and the latest prizefight. Mean-spirited squibs keep company with tender sonnets. Versified sneers co-exist with meditative lyrics and ambitious narrative poems. And the general impression is one of struggle—the lifelong inner quarrel of a poet who embraced the sacred and the profane, the cheap and the precious, in equal measure. In the early poems, an emergent spirituality wars with rural drudgery and insularity; in the middle poems, a dislocated spirit quarrels with its social environment, longing to be free in the "oriental streets of thought"; and at the end, the conflict takes still another turn, as the aging poet adopts an attitude of Olympian detachment, even as he battles with alcohol, illness, and physical decline. Through it all, one hears the antic, rebellious voice of a poet who understood tragedy well enough, but also found the "angelic absurd" in personal distress.

Kavanagh's early poems dwell on his native landscape. Undaunted by the pathetic fallacy, the poet projects his thwarted yearnings into the low drumlins and whin-hedged fields of his impoverished county:

> My black hills have never seen the sun rising,
> Eternally they look north towards Armagh.
> Lot's wife would not be salt if she had been
> Incurious as my black hills that are happy
> When dawn whitens Glassdrummond chapel.

◄←

---

[1] This is a revised edition of Kavanagh's 1972 *Complete Poems*. Explanatory notes have been added, along with "four or five pieces accidentally omitted from the first edition."

My hills hoard the bright shillings of March
While the sun searches in every pocket.
They are my Alps and I have climbed the Matterhorn
With a sheaf of hay for three perishing calves
In the field under the Big Forth of Rocksavage.

The sleety winds fondle the rushy beards of Shancoduff
While the cattle-drovers sheltering in the Featherna Bush
Look up and say: 'Who owns them hungry hills
That the water-hen and snipe must have forsaken?
A poet? Then by heavens he must be poor.'
I hear and is my heart not badly shaken?

("Shancoduff")

Shancoduff, whose name in Irish means Black Hollow, is the townland near Inniskeen where Kavanagh's sixteen-acre farm was located. Published in 1937, two years before Kavanagh left County Monaghan, this poem is a kind of elegy, an ambivalent valediction to a locale and a way of life. Artless though it seems, it deftly balances the mercantile values of the cattle-drovers against the spiritual values represented by the poet's vocation, the poet-farmer's errand of mercy, and the distant, brightening chapel. It sets plain speech against the dissonant, assonantal music of its rhymes *(happy / chapel; calves / Rocksavage)*. And, in its allusion to the story of Lot's wife, it moralizes a familiar landscape, wherein the black hills of Kavanagh's youth face away from Sodom and north towards Armagh, seat of ecclesiastical authority and spiritual power.

"For [Patrick] poetry and God were the same thing," writes Peter Kavanagh, the poet's brother, publisher, and biographer, noting that Patrick refrained from blasphemy because it would have been "unthinkable for him to insult the poetic fire, his most sacred possession and the reason for his being" (Peter Kavanagh, *Sacred Keeper*, 10). For Patrick Kavanagh, the imagination was a divine power, a gift of God and an expression of His will; and he heaped abuse on works of art that lacked "the passionate grief to

express the quintessential mind which is the angel caught in clay
. . ." and which produced, in reader or viewer, "no God-crazy
emotion" (102). Yet if Kavanagh subscribed to the Romantic con-
cept of imagination, he seldom allowed his own to wander in a
Celtic Twilight or roam far from his native soil. And if he com-
plained, in querulous moments, of his "clay-heavy mind," he
understood that his best work rose out of a closeness to daily life,
a passion to celebrate the "flower of the common light" and to
recreate "the thrill / Of common things raised up to angelhood"
("Pursuit of an Ideal").

Kavanagh's aesthetic led him to find light in stones, beauty in
potato plants, and radiance in steaming dung. It also elevated his
best work above pedestrian naturalism, lending a luminous inten-
sity to his scenes of rural Irish life. Such qualities are apparent in
his recollections of Christmas in his Monaghan parish, where the
faithful go to chapel "talking of the turkey markets / Or foreign
politics," their "plain, hard country words" becoming "Christ's
singing birds" ("Christmas Eve Remembered"). They are also evi-
dent in the two elegies he wrote for his mother, Bridget Kavanagh,
who died in November, 1945. Grief-stricken but defiant, these
poems maintain a balance of realism and romantic vision, placing
memory and imagination on an equal footing with brutal fact. In
the first elegy, the power of memory intercedes with the realities
of death and burial:

> I do not think of you lying in the wet clay
> Of a Monaghan graveyard; I see
> You walking down a lane among the poplars
> On your way to the station, or happily
>
> Going to second Mass on a summer Sunday—
> You meet me and you say:
> 'Don't forget to see about the cattle—'
> Among your earthiest words the angels stray.
>
> ("In Memory of My Mother"[I])

In the second, the pain of loss and the memory of maternal care suffuse ordinary objects and familiar gestures with an uncommon light:

> You will have the road gate open, the front door ajar
> The kettle boiling and the table set
> By the window looking out at the sycamores—
> And your loving heart lying in wait
>
> For me coming up among the poplar trees.
>
> ("In Memory of My Mother"[II])

Though verging on sentimentality, these images are braced by their unadorned directness and their fidelity to personal experience.

Similar allegiances can be felt in the textures of Kavanagh's lines. His deep distrust of formal elegance, his distaste for Yeats' idealized image of the Irish peasant, his aversion to the New Criticism and the "artificial verbalism of Richard Wilbur and his clan" —all are inscribed in the cultivated ruggedness of his rhythms, the approximations of his rhymes. Kavanagh's often-quoted statement (in "Art McCooey") that "poetry is shaped / Awkwardly but alive in the unmeasured womb" is sometimes belied by his well-turned sonnets, or by his lapses into conventional lyricism ("Coming so early / And gaysome yellow, / Oh coltsfoot blossom / You're a fine young fellow"). But on the whole he stays close to what Seamus Heaney has described as the "patterns of run and stress in the English language as it is spoken in Ireland" (*Preoccupations*, 123). In Kavanagh's comic novel *Tarry Flynn*, local speech adds color and verve, as when Tarry's mother declares, "Night, noon, and morning, it's me that's sick, sore, and sorry with the whole lot of yous." By contrast, the irregularities in Kavanagh's verse create effects of immediacy and spontaneity:

> And sometimes I am sorry when the grass
> Is growing over the stones in quiet hollows
> And the cocksfoot leans across the rutted cart-pass

That I am not the voice of country fellows
Who now are standing by some headland talking
Of turnips and potatoes or young corn
Or turf banks stripped for victory.

("Peace")

Here, as in many of Hardy's lines, it is an open question whether roughness of texture is the result of accident or conscious design. Yet I see no reason to surmise, as Seamus Heaney does, that Kavanagh's effects are not deliberate. These lines express regret at losing touch with country speech, and they might be seen as an attempt (flawed by the literary "talking / Of") to recover a countryman's voice. It is as if the potter were choosing, out of inner necessity, to work in stoneware rather than porcelain.

"Clay is the word and clay is the flesh," begins *The Great Hunger*, Kavanagh's best-known and most controversial poem. When an excerpt appeared in *Horizon* (January, 1942) its alleged blasphemy brought Dublin detectives to Kavanagh's door. Since that time, critics have not failed to find artistic faults, while acknowledging that *The Great Hunger* may be one of the great long poems of the mid-century. Beyond minor charges of myopia, static narration, and unsteadiness of focus, there is the major complaint, voiced by the poet's brother, that the narrator fails to show much concern for his main character. And there is the poet's own pronouncement, in 1960, that the *The Great Hunger* is "too strong for honesty," is "touched with hypocrisy," and "remains a tragedy" because it is "not completely reborn." "I will grant," the author sternly concludes, "that there are some remarkable things in it, but free it hardly is, for there's no laughter in it" (*November Haggard*, 15).

Kavanagh believed that tragedy is "underdeveloped comedy," and that "tragedy fully explored becomes comedy." Nowhere does he entertain a notion of tragic catharsis—or explain why we should not be moved by the plight of his bachelor farmer, Patrick

Maguire, whose sexual desires and spiritual longings do battle with inhibitions and crippling beliefs. "Who bent the coin of my destiny," Maguire cries, "That it stuck in the slot?" And in the breadth of this twenty-five-page narrative poem, spanning the seasons of Maguire's adult life, that question is thoroughly and compellingly explored, as one man's dreams of love, family, and prosperity devolve into masturbatory fantasies, vapid pub-talk, and spiritual inanition. In Kavanagh's view the blame lies largely with Maguire himself, a man enslaved to his mother, married to his land, and betrayed by an other-worldly Christianity which fails to recognize that "God is in the bits and pieces of Everyday" and that "God's truth is life—even the grotesque shapes of his foulest fire." But Maguire's destiny is also that of the parish, the region, the Catholic peasantry in general; and the withering power of the Church may be observed within its own demesne:

> Like the afterbirth of a cow stretched on a branch in the wind
> Life dried in the veins of these women and men:
> The grey and grief and unlove,
> The bones in the backs of their hands,
> And the chapel pressing its low ceiling over them.

(IX)

"For the strangled impulse," the narrator reminds us, "there is no redemption."

Yet there is perhaps more spiritual freedom in *The Great Hunger* than its author was disposed to acknowledge. At points that freedom is more asserted than demonstrated, as when we are told that Maguire's neighbors "sometimes . . . did laugh and see the sunlight, / A narrow slice of divine instruction" (IX). But elsewhere we experience the imaginative freedom of the narrator as he pleads on behalf of the rural poor:

> Let us be kind, let us be kind and sympathetic:
> Maybe life is not for joking or finding happiness in—

This tiny light in Oriental darkness
Looking out chance windows of poetry or prayer.

And the grief and defeat of men like these peasants
Is God's way—maybe—and we must not want too much
To see.
The twisted thread is stronger than the wind-swept fleece.
And in the end who shall rest in truth's high peace?

(XI)

Here the narrator's precise trope—the twisted thread—and his fluent rhythms evoke a sense of release, however fleeting. And, unlike Maguire's escapist daydreams, the narrator's speech creates a Jacob's ladder, mediating between earthbound poverty and heavenly grace.

The Great Hunger marks the high point of Kavanagh's mid-career. *Lough Derg*, written in the same year, is similarly ambitious but not nearly as good. It contains some fine sonnets in the form of pilgrims' prayers, but on the whole it suffers from the besetting illness of Kavanagh's middle period, namely his tendency to turn editorialist, to decline into journalistic prose:

Beside St. Brigid's Cross—an ancient relic
A fragment of the Middle Ages set
Into the modern masonry of the conventional Basilica . . .
+ + +
Lough Derg overwhelmed the individual imagination
And the personal tragedy.
Only God thinks of the dying sparrow
In the middle of a war.

In these lines, as in his squibs on Jack Doyle, F.J. McCormick, "Jack Yeats' New Novel," and other ephemeral subjects, Kavanagh settles for slack language ("an ancient relic") and drastically narrowed vision. Often his tone is acerbic, as in "The Paddiad," the best of his satirical verses. But on the whole Kavanagh's satire lacks both the scope and the bite of his Augustan forbears, and it seldom rises above topical sniping.

Had Kavanagh's career ended with his poems of the forties, it would have presented posterity with a sad and all-too-familiar spectacle. Fortunately, his descent into self-indulgent satire was followed by a resurgence of his talent and a return to the rigors of the sonnet. Kavanagh made much of his "rebirth" in August, 1955, which occurred as he lay on the bank of Dublin's Grand Canal, recuperating from major surgery:

> All reports from everywhere are the same reports. I want to report about the Grand Canal bank last summer. I report on the part of the bank just to the west of Baggot Street Bridge. Most days last summer in the beautiful heat I lay there on the grass with only my shirt and trousers on. I lay on that grass in an ante-natal roll with a hand under my head. . . . I learned the pleasures of being passive. The green still water, the light around gables.
>
> (November Haggard, 44, 85)

What he learned, or gained, was freedom from ambition and egocentric attachments. And if his prose accounts of this experience sometimes protest too much, his late sonnets, written under its influence, offer convincing proof:

> O commemorate me where there is water,
> Canal water preferably, so stilly
> Greeny at the heart of summer. Brother
> Commemorate me thus beautifully
> Where by a lock Niagarously roars
> The falls for those who sit in the tremendous silence
> Of mid-July. No one will speak in prose
> Who finds his way to these Parnassian islands.
> A swan goes by head low with many apologies,
> Fantastic light looks through the eyes of bridges—
> And look! A barge comes bringing from Athy
> And other far-flung towns mythologies.

> O commemorate me with no hero-courageous
> Tomb—just a canal-bank seat for the passer-by.
>
> ("Lines Written on a Seat on the Grand Canal, Dublin,
> 'Erected to the Memory of Mrs. Dermot O'Brien'")

Given the ease and grace of this sonnet, its generosity and quiet drollery, it may be churlish to complain of its diction—"stilly/greeny" is distracting, "tremendous silence" close to banal—or to detect vestigial vanity in the rejected, heroic memorial. As an expression of beatific receptivity, the poem is fully and movingly achieved.

The other Canal Bank sonnets (especially "Canal Bank Walk" and "Come Dance with Kitty Stobling") possess similar virtues, and together these poems represent Kavanagh's last major achievement. More poems followed, but none had the same serenity or power. Kavanagh quoted, with approval, Rilke's remark that a lifetime's experience might produce a few enduring lines, and though Kavanagh himself produced more than his share of memorable lyrics, it may be some time before his canon can be established and his stature measured. Seamus Heaney suggests that in *The Great Hunger* Kavanagh sounded "an Irish note that is not dependent on backward looks towards the Irish tradition"; and Dillon Johnston, an American authority on Irish verse, credits Kavanagh with dismantling, once and for all, the romantic myth of the Irish peasant. Those are not small accomplishments, and it is little wonder that Irish poets as diverse as Heaney, John Montague, and Paul Muldoon have expressed admiration for Kavanagh and acknowledged his influence on their development.

Whether the world beyond Ireland will commemorate Kavanagh—or afford him the stature of Yeats or Synge—remains to be seen, but signs are beginning to point in that direction. In January, 1985, the Guggenheim Museum hosted a celebration of Kavanagh's work, with readings by Galway Kinnell, Louis Simpson, and Peter Kavanagh. And in recent years, poets and scholars from Europe, England, and the United States have descended on the village of Inniskeen, visiting Kavanagh's grave and tramping up the boreens to see the black hills the poet renounced, the fields he found so stifling. The irony is apt, as is the tribute. For, as Kavanagh tells us in *The Green Fool* (1938), the autobiography he later debunked: "I wasn't really a writer. I had seen a strange beautiful light on the hills and that was all."

1986

Lyric Memory

TO THE SORROWS of modern Ireland John Montague has brought an historian's understanding and a harper's delicate music. He has kept faith with his lyric gift while bearing witness to violent events. Born in Brooklyn in 1929, thirteen years after the Easter Rising and nine years after partition, Montague might have preferred a contemplative's detachment, had history not thrust him into the roles of activist, elegist, and interpreter of political upheaval. An internationalist at heart, he has accepted the nationalist's mantle reluctantly, in the manner of an exile rather than a native son, but he has worn it with distinction. In three book-length sequences of poems (*The Rough Field*, 1972; *The Great Cloak*, 1978; *The Dead Kingdom*, 1984) he has told a painful personal story—a tale of dislocation, loss, separation, and renewal. Beyond that, he has told the story of Northern Ireland as no other poet has, tracing the present sectarian violence to its roots in Jacobean Ulster. Wary of the "lyric memory" that would "soften the fact" ("Dancehall"), he has sought "exactness," employing a "low-pitched style" that will not "betray the event." Yet his quiet music has persisted, braced and chastened by its encounters with civil strife.

Montague's *Selected Poems* (Wake Forest, 1982) gathers the work of six previous collections. Its earliest poem dates from 1952, its most recent from the early eighties. Montague's diverse

subjects include mummers, wartime prison camps, cherished land-
scapes and troublesome mythologies, monastic relics and Gaelic
antiquities, oracular elders and loving aunts. His abiding themes
are loss and recurrence ("With all my circling a failure to return"),
and his dominant tone is elegiac. But when his thoughts turn to
matters of politics and religion, his fluent voice grows harsh. For
Montague is an Ulster Catholic, a Northern Republican, reared
on a farm in the townland of Garvaghey in Co. Tyrone. As he
communes with his ancestors, or surveys the "shards of a lost tra-
dition," conciliatory talk gives way to bitter anger. Legacies of
dispossession perturb his contemplative calm:

> This bitterness
> I inherit from my father, the
> swarm of blood
> to the brain, the vomit surge
> of race hatred,
> the victim seeing the oppressor,
> bold Jacobean
> planter, or gadget laden marine,
> who has scatter-
> ed his household gods, used
> his people
> as servants, flushed his women
> like game.

("Sound of a Wound")

Montague's gentler poems reclaim his rural boyhood. Their
setting is the North of Ireland, west of the Bann. Their era is the
thirties and forties, when electrification and mechanization were
altering the Irish countryside. In a recent interview, Montague
regretted the loss of small farms like his family's at Garvaghey,
which have been replaced by large-scale factory farms, with their
"little white eggs" and "hormone-plumped beef." At the same
time, he acknowledged that farm life of the thirties was often bru-

tal, that "people died early." And, in any event, bulldozers have long since reshaped the "hedged, hillocky / Tyrone grassland," producing such developments as the new Omagh Highway—and stripping away the objects of nostalgia.

Montague's realism steadies his backward looks, where the obvious risks are triteness and sentimentality. At times, his lyric memory does get the better of him, as in his sentimental eulogy for Tim, "the first horse I rode / seasick on his barrel back" ("Tim"), or in his pastel sketches of the Irish peasantry:

> 'I like to look across', said
> Barney Horisk, leaning on his *slean*,
> 'And think of all the people
> Who have bin.'
>
> ("The Road's End")

Yet, in his stronger poems, Montague takes a sterner look, as he chronicles such changes as the replacement of horses by machines, the "bulky harness and sucking step" giving way to the tractor's noise and smoke. Rather than mourn the people who have been, or sigh for the farmer leaning on his turf spade, these poems look clearly and steadily at rural life:

> In the girdered dark
> of the byre, cattle move;
> warm engines hushed
> to a siding groove
>
> before the switch flicks
> down for milking.
> In concrete partitions
> they rattle their chains
>
> while the farmhand eases
> rubber tentacles to tug
> lightly but rhythmically
> on their swollen dugs
> ◄+

and up the pale cylinders
of the milking machine
mounts an untouched
steadily pulsing stream.

Only the tabby steals
to dip its radar whiskers
with old-fashioned relish
in a chipped saucer

and before Seán lurches
to kick his boots off
in the night-silent kitchen
he draws a mug of froth

to settle on the sideboard
under the hoard of delft.
A pounding transistor shakes
the Virgin on her shelf

as he dreams toward bed.
A last glance at a magazine,
he puts the mug to his head,
grunts, and drains it clean.

("A Drink of Milk")

These lines owe something to Patrick Kavanagh, who taught
Montague's generation to value the common life of the parish. At
the same time, they share little of Kavanagh's Catholic mysticism,
and they reveal an affinity with William Carlos Williams, whom
Montague met while studying at Iowa City in the mid-fifties. The
domestic surroundings, the sharp visual details, and the colloqui-
al idiom recall Williams's shorter poems; and though Montague's
setting is remote, in spirit he is not far from Williams's cat climb-
ing over the jamcloset or his "poor old woman" eating plums on
the street. What sets Montague's version apart is its backward
look, its muted wit, and its adventurous use of traditional form.

Homely images grow bright within the confines of irregular quatrains and imperfect rhymes. Compressed syntax heightens the plain diction of the closing stanza.

Elsewhere, Montague looks much further back, as he ponders the depths of the Gaelic past. Often Montague allows the past to interrogate the present, or vice versa, as in "Old Mythologies," where a "whole dormitory of heroes turn over" in their graves, "regretting their butchers' days." Elsewhere, he gazes with reverence at the regions of the Gaeltacht, where the ancient ways have been preserved, and the mellifluous Irish language, however threatened, is still intact. Like Pearse Hutchinson, Paul Muldoon, and other postwar Irish poets who write in English, Montague often introduces Irish words and phrases, invoking what Donoghue has called the "true voice of feeling" for an Irish poet. "*Tá an Ghaedilg againn arís*," intones a speaker in "A Lost Tradition," chanting a "rusty litany of praise": "We have the Irish again."

It is not easy for an American reader to separate the strands of nationalistic sentiment and original perception in Montague's encounters with Gaelic culture. As director of Claddagh Records, Montague has been active in the revival of traditional Irish music, and he has written a moving elegy for Seán O'Riada, the Irish composer. At the same time, he has stood apart from the narrow ideologies of Irish nationalism, and in his best work a romantic vision of Ireland, derived from Patrick Pearse and Eamon de Valera, co-exists with a skeptic's sense of history. In "A Grafted Tongue," an Irish schoolchild of the post-Famine years weeps as he attempts to learn the King's English:

> After each mistake
>
>   the master
> gouges another mark
> on the tally stick
> hung about its neck
>
>   Like a bell

on a cow, a hobble
on a straying goat . . .

    Decades later
that child's grandchild's
speech stumbles over lost
syllables of an old order.

And in "The Answer," the poet visits a cottage on the Dingle
Peninsula, where the woman of the house proffers "the ritual
greetings":

*   Dia dhuit /*
*   Dia agus Muire dhuit /*
*   Dia agus Muire*
agus Padraig dhuit

          invocation of powers
to cleanse the mind.
              Then the question
and the answer.
         'What did she say?'
I was asked when I came back to the car
but could only point the way
over the hill to where
        obscured in sea
mist, the small, grey stones of the oratory
held into the Atlantic for a thousand years.

Here the speaker, a lapsed Catholic asking for directions to the
Gallarus Oratory, receives a blessing ("God—Mary and Patrick
—to you"). This encounter with the "old way, / the way of cour-
tesy," and with the thousand-year-old culture embodied in its lan-
guage, leaves the modern, secular poet speechless.

    It is characteristic of Montague to give the speaking part—the
voice of the ancient culture—to a woman, especially an elderly,
Irish-speaking woman. The hag or *cailleach* is a familiar figure in

Irish poetry, but in Montague's poems it is a recurrent motif, akin to Yeats's winding stair or tower. Whether she take the form of the Sean Bhean Bhocht (the poor old woman), "eyes rheumy with racial memory," or an aged matriarch, "jowls weathered past yellow to old gold," or the Hag of Beare in Montague's fine translation of the ninth-century poem, this fearsome woman haunts Montague's imagination, both as a repository of wisdom and as a symbol of ancient cultural constraints. Nowhere is Montague's skeptical sensibility, his resistance to romantic mythologies, more fully tested than in his meditations on these archetypal figures.

In the most powerful of these poems, a narrative describing the attempted rape of an elderly cottager by a drunken intruder, the *cailleach* is an old woman of Garvaghey, one of the "dolmens round [the poet's] childhood." As a boy, the speaker was frightened by her "great hooked nose" and "mottled claws." Now in his manhood, he is moved by the terrible story she confides:

> In the darkness
> they wrestle, two creatures crazed
> with loneliness, the smell of the
> decaying cottage in his nostrils
> like a drug, his body heavy on hers,
> the tasteless trunk of a seventy-year-
> old virgin, which he rummages while
> she battles for life
>
>   bony fingers
> searching desperately to push
> against his bull neck. 'I prayed
> to the blessed Virgin herself
> for help and after a time
> I broke his grip.'
>
>   He rolls
> to the floor, snores asleep,

while she cowers until dawn
and the dogs' whimpering starts
him awake, to lurch back across
the wet bog.

("The Wild Dog Rose")

Bizarre and mysterious as this story is, its power derives largely
from its understated naturalism. Montague's exact descriptions,
strong enjambments ("of the / decaying"; "seventy-year- / old
virgin"), and condensed phrasing ("snores asleep"; "cowers until
dawn") counter any tendency toward melodrama or mystifica-
tion. We are in the eerie precincts of the bogs, to be sure, but we
are very far from the mists of the Celtic Twilight.

"It's a great pity," Montague has remarked (in the interview
cited earlier) "that we gave up the storytelling aspects of poetry
. . . Shakespeare's full of stories; even Spenser, whom as a man I
detest, has some splendid stories . . ." Montague is himself an
accomplished writer of short stories, with one collection (*Death of
a Chieftain*, 1964) to his credit and another in the making. In his
verse he has shied away from the long narrative poem, but he has
shown a liking for the shorter forms of narrative—the anecdote,
parable, or fable. His forte is not the intricate plot but the radiant
detail, the image that tells the story. In "Witness," an opening
stanza creates a rich, sharply defined interior:

By the crumbling fire we talked
Animal-dazed by the heat
While the lawyer unhooked a lamp
From peat blackened rafters
And climbed the circle of stairs.

In "A Lost Tradition," place-names and visual details, carefully
chosen, recreate a tragic moment in Irish history:

Tír Eoghain: Land of Owen,
Province of the O'Niall;

The ghostly tread of O'Hagan's
Barefoot gallowglasses marching
To merge forces in Dun Geanainn

Push southward to Kinsale!
Loudly the war-cry is swallowed
In swirls of black rain and fog
As Ulster's pride, Elizabeth's foemen,
Founder in a Munster bog.

Within the compass of two stanzas, Montague evokes the defeat of
Hugh O'Neill's forces at Kinsale in 1601, which precipitated the
Flight of the Earls (1607) and augured the end of the Gaelic social
order. *The Rough Field*, from which "A Lost Tradition" has been
extracted, tells that story in much greater detail, but the method
remains the same. Fragments and anecdotes, artfully arranged, do
the work of continuous narrative. Historical moments are
glimpsed through the loopholes of well-made lyric poems.

   Montague employs similar means in his dealings with the pre-
sent violence in the North. Here, however, his manner and his
intent are sometimes at odds. For if his impressions of Derry and
Belfast, rendered through brittle images and truncated syntax,
create a sense of political chaos and sectarian fragmentation, his
general intent is to create a healing vision, a balanced and inte-
grated whole. "A New Siege" records the struggle in Belfast:

> Lines of suffering
>   lines of defeat
> under the walls
>   ghetto terraces
> sharp pallor of
>   unemployed shades
>
> slope shouldered
>   broken bottles
> pubs and bookies

>   red brick walls
>   Falls or Shankhill

But in "The Unpartitioned Intellect," an eloquent plea for an
open sensibility and a united Ireland, Montague renounces the
"partitioned intellect" represented, on the one side, by de Valera
and the Gaelic Athletic Association, and, on the other, by Ian
Paisley and the Orange Order. In its place he would have "a sen-
sibility which is prepared to entertain, to be sympathetic to, all the
traditions of which our country can be said to be composed."
Its emblem would be the harp of the United Irishmen. Its sym-
bol would be the Irish poet Francis Ledwidge (1891-1917),
who mourned the execution of one of the leaders of the Easter
Rising, while "wearing the British army uniform in which he was
to die. . . ." ("The Unpartitioned Intellect," in *Irish Writers and
Society at Large*, ed. Masaru Sekine, Colin Smythe, 1985).

Montague has acknowledged his "ferocious Republican back-
ground," and in the imagery of *The Rough Field* at least one crit-
ic (George Watson, in Sekine, *op.cit.*) has found a Catholic racial
myth and a nationalist's biased history. Nevertheless, Montague's
plea for tolerance rings as true as the strident complaints he has
uttered elsewhere; and his many love poems express an emotion
equal to sectarian hatred. Born and bred a partisan, he has not
shrunk from the national debate, but he has also shown a capaci-
ty for disengagement and impartial detachment. Such is his per-
spective in "What a View," where a fictive seagull looks down on
the rifts in Garvaghey:

>   He would be lost,
>   my seagull, to see
>   why the names on
>
>   one side of the street
>   (MacAteer, Carney)
>   are Irish and ours
>   ◄◄

and the names across
(Carnew, MacCrea)
are English and theirs . . .

and if a procession,
Orange or Hibernian,
came stepping through

he would hear the
same thin, scrannel
note, under the drums.

In another poet this vision might seem culpably Olympian—or
naively utopian. A detractor might object that the MacCreas are
by now as Irish as the MacAteers, and that such distinctions per-
petuate the divisions they purport to mend. Yet in a poet as
grounded in history as Montague, as attuned to his country's
intractable quarrels, this gentle fantasy has healing powers. "More
substance in our enmities," wrote Yeats, "than in our love." To
such pessimism Montague's sturdy, curative voice offers a strong
rejoinder.[1]

1987

---

[1] Mr. Montague was interviewed by Earl Ingersoll and Ben Howard in
Brockport, New York, on October 4, 1985. The interview is printed in *The Literary
Review* (vol. 31, no. 1, Fall 1987, 23–31).

Home from Home[1]

EXILE IS the birthright of the Irish poet. It is rooted in his poetic traditions and embedded in the language or languages he speaks. "Most of them speak English," writes Denis Donoghue of contemporary Irish poets, "but they have a sense, just barely acknowledged, that the true voice of feeling speaks in Irish, not a dead language like Latin but a banished language, a voice in exile." Today many younger Irish poets write in their native language, knowing full well that it is a dying tongue. Others, like Paul Muldoon, Medbh McGuckian, and Seamus Heaney, write in English, while delving into the Irish lineages of English words. Yet all share the uneasiness of living in a fractured society, a post-colonial collage, where the erstwhile oppressor's speech prevails, and the "true voice of feeling" survives precariously in remote areas of the West. To write exclusively in Irish is to banish oneself from the larger literary world. But to write in English alone is to dispossess oneself of a centuries-old tradition.

Derek Mahon grew up in Belfast, Northern Ireland, but like Louis MacNeice, his literary forbear, he has lived most of his adult life in Europe, removed from both the Troubles and the

---

[1] Derek Mahon, *The Hunt by Night*, Wake Forest University Press, 1983; *Courtyards in Delft*, Gallery Books (Dublin), 1981; and *Poems 1962–1978*, Oxford University Press, 1979.

beauty of his native province. In many of his poems, Mahon looks downward through layers of natural history, or outward toward Europe and America, or forward into a distant future. But like any exile, he also looks homeward:

> Tonight, their simple church grown glamorous,
> The proud parishioners of the outlying parts
> Lift up their hymn-books and their hearts
> To please the outside-broadcast cameras.
> The darkness deepens; day draws to a close;
> A well-bred sixth-former yawns with her nose.
>
> Outside, the hymn dies among rocks and dunes.
> Conflicting rhythms of the incurious sea,
> Not even contemptuous of these tiny tunes,
> Take over where our thin ascriptions fail.
> Down there the silence of the laboratory,
> Trombone dispatches of the beleaguered whale.
>
> Never look back, they said; but they were wrong.
> The zinc wave-dazzle after a night of rain,
> A washed-out sky humming with stars, the mist
> And echoing fog-horns of the soul, belong
> To our lost lives. We must be born again,
> As the gable-ends of the seaside towns insist;
>
> And so we were, to look back constantly
> On that harsh landscape and its procreant sea,
> Bitter and curative, as tonight we did,
> Listening to our own nearly-voices chime
> In the parochial lives we might have led,
> Praising a stony god who died before our time.
>
> ("'Songs of Praise'")

This graceful meditation represents Mahon's mature style, and it also sounds his abiding themes. It is characteristic of Mahon to set human creations against the humbling presence of the natural world and to contrast man-made orders with the enduring rhythms of the elements. Here these familiar contrasts are given fresh life, not only by the poem's precise diction, but also by the speaker's complex relationship to the scene. He is both chorister and visitor, exile and native son, who distances himself even as he speaks. The deft rhymes (*glamorous/cameras*), the mimicry of "proud parishioners," the zeugma of "hymn-books" and "hearts," the punning "beleaguered" and the etymological by-play of "parishioner" and "parochial"—all set the urbane speaker at arm's length from the life he might have led. At once an insider and an outsider, Mahon adopts a perspective he elsewhere describes as "theoptic," placing the "tiny tunes" and seaside houses against the backdrop of oceanic music.

Mahon thinks often of the lives he might have led. In two decades and five full-length collections, he has addressed a wide range of friends, artists, poets, and historical personages, including De Quincey, Van Gogh, Paul Durcan, Pasternak, Joyce, Mac-Neice, and Malcolm Lowry. Often his vehicle is the dedication, or the imitation, or variations on a line from an earlier poet. For his sustained meditations on loss, decay, entropy, and the inefficacy of art, he has also turned to the Horatian verse epistle, taking Pope and Auden as his guides:

> Portstewart, Portrush, Portballintrae—
> *Un beau pays mal habité*,
> Policed by rednecks in dark cloth
> And roving gangs of tartan youth.
> No place for a gentleman like you.
> The good, the beautiful and the true
> Have a tough time of it; and yet
> There *is* that rather obvious sunset,
>
> And a strange poetry of decay
> Charms the senile hotels by day,

While in the small hours the rattle
Of a cat knocking over a milk bottle
On a distant doorstep by moonlight
Can set you thinking half the night.

("The Sea in Winter")

Here, as in Auden's "New Year Letter," disciplined rhymes
impart an air of public formality to colloquial speech, and com-
plex syntax lends weight to an offhand manner. Yet, under
Mahon's aegis, the verse letter becomes less a vehicle for social
criticism than a mode of lyrical utterance; and the form that for
Pope served a didactic purpose becomes an outlander's commu-
niqué, an exile's cry. In the lines just quoted, Mahon endeavors to
bridge the distance between his northern Irish outpost and the
"white island in the south," where his friend and recipient,
Desmond O'Grady, is writing poems, drinking retsina, and enjoy-
ing Mediterranean amenities. In another verse letter, "Beyond
Howth Head," Mahon makes a similar effort, as he writes from
Monkstown, Co. Dublin, to a friend in London:

The pros outweigh the cons that glow
From Beckett's bleak *reductio*—
And who would trade self-knowledge for
A prelapsarian metaphor,
Love-play of the ironic conscience
For a prescriptive innocence?
'Lewde libertie', whose midnight work
Disturbed the peace of Co. Cork

And fired Kilcolman's windows when
The flower of Ireland looked to Spain,
Come back and be with us again!
But take a form that sheds for love
That tight-arsed, convent-bred disdain
The whole wide world knows nothing of;

> And flash, an *aisling*, through the dawn
> Where Yeats's hill-men still break stone.

These allusive lines express a complex longing. Mindful of Beckett's nihilistic vision, Mahon weighs the discomforts of self-awareness against naive felicity. While opting for irony and modern skepticism, he also evokes Edmund Spenser's sixteenth-century Ireland, calling up the ghosts of Irish rebellion. From the vantage point of Spenser's Castle Kilcolman in Co. Cork, the specter of liberty looked threatening and "lewde." But to Mahon that specter is a version of the *aisling*, the vision of a young woman symbolizing Irish freedom. As Mahon entertains that vision he invites the forces of liberty to penetrate Irish insularity and religious repression. Yet he also recalls Parnell's words to a common laborer: "Ireland shall get her freedom and you still break stone."

Mahon's own sense of freedom—and his wish to inhabit "the whole wide world"—is evident in everything he writes. He will consider "everything that is the case imaginatively" ("Tractatus"), often by entering the lives and times of other exiled writers. His many personae include Knut Hamsun, De Quincey, Brecht, Ovid, and (in his imitations) Horace, Rimbaud, Pasternak, Cavafy, and Nerval. Possessed of a rich historical imagination, Mahon can recreate Brecht's Svendborg, where the poet lives in precarious exile from Hitler's Germany, hearing "screams beyond the frontier." He can reconstruct the tranquility of seventeenth-century Delft, where he observes "oblique light on the trite, on brick and tile . . ." ("Courtyards in Delft"). In "Ovid in Tomis," however, he adopts a bolder strategy. Like Geoffrey Hill's Offa (in *Mercian Hymns*) Mahon's Ovid is an ahistorical figure, a spirit of exile spanning twenty centuries. His tone is not so much mournful as serio-comic:

> No doubt, in time
> To come, this huddle of
> Mud huts will be
> ◄┼

A handsome city,
An important port,
A popular resort,

With an oil pipeline,
Martini terraces
And even a dignified

Statue of *me*
Gazing out to sea
From the promenade;

But for the moment
It is merely a place
Where I have to be.

A far cry from Ovid's own plaintive *Tristia*, Mahon's poem takes
a global and philosophical view of the poet's condition, remind-
ing us that exile is not peculiar to any one century or nationality.
Nor does it lack historical ironies.

Mahon often gives the impression that he would prefer to live
outside of history altogether, whether through removal to some
remote locale, or through the grace of timeless art. His geograph-
ical retreats are usually northern, sparsely populated places—
Portstewart, Rathlin Island, Co. Donegal—where "the long glow
leaps from the dark soil," and the nightmare of history can be
temporarily forgotten. In Donegal the hills are a "deeper green /
than anywhere in the world," and "the light / Of heaven" plays
upon the mountains. At Portrush, in Co. Antrim, the north wind
"whistles off the stars" and "choirs now and forever." And though
the poet may be living in comfortable urban surroundings, his spir-
itual home and his standard of value lie in those austere environs:

A dream of limestone in sea light
Where gulls have placed their perfect prints.
Reflection in that final sky
Shames vision into simple sight;

Into pure sense, experience.
Atlantic leagues away tonight,
Conceived beyond such innocence,
I clutch the memory still, and I
Have measured everything with it since.

("Thinking of Inishere in Cambridge, Massachusetts")

Elsewhere Mahon projects his yearnings into the faces of watchers on a Canadian beach, who "dream of other islands, / Clear cliffs and salt water . . . / Redemption in a wind or a tide" ("April on Toronto Island").

Mahon finds another kind of solace in the changeless world of art, whether it be that of "an old man in Bognor Regis / Making dreadnoughts out of matches" or, more often, the intricate works or European masters. Among contemporary poets writing in English, Mahon is one of a handful who can write convincingly and even movingly about European paintings, perhaps because he finds, in the images of Munch, De Hooch, Uccello, and others, a reflection of his own obsessions. In "The Hunt by Night," based on Uccello's fifteenth-century painting, he contrasts the tame and playful ethos of the painting with the primitive reality of the hunt. In "Courtyards in Delft," based on De Hooch, he views well-scrubbed yards with apprehension, perceiving repressed savagery beneath the Reformation spirit. Yet, whatever tensions they may express, and whatever violence they may contain, these paintings provide a respite from historical process, a "composure / Of painted surfaces." For Mahon, as for Keats, "Every artefact" presents

A pure, self-referential act,
That the intolerant soul may be
Retrieved from triviality
And the locked heart, so long in pawn
To steel, redeemed by wood and stone.

("Another Sunday Morning")

Of course, the cure is only temporary, and for Mahon it is also suspect. "Somewhere," he conjectures, "beyond the scorched gable and the burnt-out buses / there is a poet indulging / his wretched rage for order" ("Rage for Order"). What his indulgence produces is, at best, an "eddy of semantic scruples / in an unstructurable sea." At its worst, it is "obsolete bumf"; and, as its creator ponders its worth, he is left in a state of radical doubt:

> And all the time I have my doubts
> About this verse-making. The shouts
> Of souls in torment round the town
> At closing time make as much sense
> And carry as much significance
> As these lines carefully set down.
> All farts in a biscuit tin, in truth—
> Faint cries, sententious or uncouth.
>
> ("The Sea in Winter")

Yet, for all his self-deprecating realism, Mahon admits to a need, now and in the future, for the poet's "desperate ironies." Poems provide the long views, the "theoptic" perspectives that make the present more endurable. As if to atone for his "indulgence" in verse, Mahon offers his own perspectives on contemporary realities, including the privations of gypsies in their caravans, the desolation of the housing estates, the "terrier-taming, garden-watering" boredom of the suburbs, and the sectarian violence of Derry and Belfast. When not satiric or ironic, his tone is reflective and consolatory:

> What of the change envisioned here,
> The quantum leap from fear to fire?
> Smoke from a thousand chimneys strains
> One way beneath the returning rains
> That shroud the bomb-sites, while the fog
> Of time receives the ideologue.

A Russian freighter bound for home
Mourns to the city in its gloom.

("Derry Morning")

If this is more soothing than convincing, more lulling than reveal-
ing, it is perhaps because we cannot yet take the long view Mahon
urges, or distance ourselves so readily. Whether in Derry or
Beirut, the ideologue seems all too prepared to step out of the fog
and commit some new atrocity.

Mahon's poems on the Troubles remind us that tribal feuds and
age-old grievances lie close to the heart of any Irish poet, exiled
or otherwise. At the same time, it would be a mistake to think of
Mahon as an "Ulster poet" or to view his concerns as peculiarly
Irish. When he chooses to train his satiric rhetoric on Ulster
Calvinists, he can be devastating, but for the most part, he remains
the international exile, shriven of nostalgia or partisan involve-
ment. In one recent poem, "The Globe in North Carolina,"
Mahon's customary distance reaches a new extreme, as he views
the earth from somewhere in space, and addresses his own planet
as if it were a faraway god:

> Veined marble, if we only knew,
> In practice as in theory, true
> Salvation lies not in the thrust
> Of action only, but the trust
> We place in our peripheral
> Night garden in the glory-hole
> Of space, a home from home, and what
> Devotion we can bring to it!

Such musings may strike us as escapist, but they suggest an alter-
native to what Mahon, in the same poem, calls "era-provincial
self-regard." As he projects himself out of his own time, Mahon
envisions a world wherein skepticism and irony, "grown trite,"
will be "dumb / Before the new thing that must come . . ." That

is a surprising affirmation—and a startling leap of faith. In another poet it might seem merely wistful, but in a poet like Derek Mahon, born to wear the *eiron's* mask and the exile's guise, it carries the force of prophetic vision.

1986

Articulating the Silences

IF YEATS WAS the bard of the Irish Big House, Eavan Boland is the poet of suburban twilight. Formal in manner and delicate in feeling, her poems gravitate toward the "in-between / neither here-nor-there hour of evening," the zones of anticipation and aftertaste, "what is left of / a mouth after kissing," or "the ache of things ending in the jasmine darkening early." Whether her setting is the kitchen, the nursery, or the suburban garden, Boland endeavors to "bless the ordinary" and "sanctify the common," be it the "white iron of the garden chair," or a greenhouse "rank with the best / Irish tomatoes." At their most sumptuous, her poems celebrate the variousness of plants, foods, furnishings, and fabrics, while releasing the resonances of common things. At their most austere, they maintain a cool aloofness, bathing their subjects in "the hard shyness of Atlantic light."

Eavan Boland was born in Dublin in 1944. The present collection,[1] handsomely produced, represents the work of her early middle years. Along with fifty-eight lyric poems she has included two ambitious sequences, "Outside History" and "Domestic Interior," the first reflecting on the self in history and the second exploring the dynamics of marriage and motherhood. Writing in a jagged minimalist style inherited from Plath ("In a ringed / coiling, / a

---

[1] *Outside History: Selected Poems 1980–1990.* Norton, 1991.

convulsion, / I will heave / to a sinuous / and final / shining off / of skin:") or in an elegant descriptive style reminiscent of Elizabeth Bishop, Boland entertains a copious variety of themes, including Irish history and legend, domestic malaise, cultural dislocation, marriage, childhood, womanhood, and the tensions between language and experience. Whatever her subject, her professed aim is to reveal the truth of her feelings, resisting on the one side the pressure of feminist separatism, which would have her "discard the complexities of true feeling for the relative simplicity of anger," and on the other, the claims of what she has called the "Romantic Heresy," which would exalt the privileged moment at the expense of ordinary life. For Boland, the female poet is an artist "caught in a field of force," with separatist ideology urging her to "disregard the whole poetic past as patriarchal betrayal," and the Romantic heresy dismissing domestic, marital, and parental experience as unpoetic. ("The Woman Poet: Her Dilemma," *American Poetry Review*, January/February 1987). Her challenge is to resist those pressures while not ignoring them—and to be true to her own experience, however domestic or ordinary.

As an Irish poet Boland must contend with two other potent forces, namely those of Irish history and the Irish poetic tradition. For the most part, Boland's poems steer clear of political and religious issues. They make no mention of sectarian politics or the Troubles over the border. At the same time, they bear the weight of the Irish past—that "palsy of regrets," as Boland calls it. "I won't go back to it," she declares in "Mise Eire," renouncing the "land of the Gulf Stream, / the small farm, / the scalded memory, / the songs / that bandage up the history, / the words / that make a rhythm of the crime / where time is time past." And yet she does go back, time and again, both in her themes and attitudes and, more subtly, in the rhythms of her lines. Boland has acknowledged her emotional and literary debts to Patrick Kavanagh, who demonstrated a "fierce attachment to the devalued parts of his experience," and even more to Yeats, who "stumbled into tragedies and limitations" and brought a "powerful, volatile sense of humiliation . . . into the great monolith of poetry" (*Irish Literary Supplement*, Fall 1988). Her felt affinity for Yeats can be discerned in her formality, her sculpted phrases, her arm's-length distance from her subjects. Now and then, it can also be heard in the cadences of her lines:

> The chimneys have been swept.
> The gardens have their winter cut.
> The shrubs are prinked, the hedges gelded.
> ("Suburban Woman: A Detail")

For all its plainness, this passage calls to mind "The Wild Swans at Coole" ("The trees are in their autumn beauty, / The woodland paths are dry") and seems almost a *contrafactum* of Yeats's lines.

Beyond the specific precedent of Yeats or Kavanagh, the Irish influence may be more broadly discerned in Boland's vexed concern with language, her retrospective and realistic outlook, her elegiac view of history, and her pervasive sense of exile. In "The Emigrant Irish" she reflects on her ancestry, while plucking the dusty harp of Irish lamentation:

> What they survived we could not even live.
> By their lights now it is time to
> imagine how they stood there, what they stood with,
> that their possessions may become our power:
>
> Cardboard. Iron. Their hardships parceled in them.
> Patience. Fortitude. Long-suffering
> in the bruise-colored dusk of the New World.

Invoking the pathos of "Galway Bay" and other immigrant ballads, this slow lament expresses its author's own sense of exile and spiritual dislocation. The daughter of a diplomat, Boland spent

much of her childhood away from Ireland, and in her reminis-
cences she looks back with bitterness at a time

> when all of England to an Irish child

> was nothing more than what you'd lost and how:
> was the teacher in the London convent who,
> when I produced "I amn't" in the classroom
> turned and said—"you're not in Ireland now."
>
> ("An Irish Childhood in England: 1951")

Nursing an old hurt, the poet voices a national grievance, a post-
colonial remonstrance.

Turning to her present, domestic life, Boland expresses strong
but ambivalent feelings. In tones ranging from the resigned to the
desperate, the wistful to the indignant, she portrays herself as an
assiduous laundress, seamstress, quilter, and cook, companioned
by appliances and attuned to domestic routine. In a few crisp
phrases she defines her work and her world:

> crossing between
> the garden and the house,
> under the whitebeam trees
> keeping an eye on
> the length of the grass,
> the height of the hedge,
> the distance of the children

> I am Chardin's woman

> edged in reflected light,
> hardened by
> the need to be ordinary.
>
> ("Self-Portrait on a Summer Evening")

"Am I," the poet asks, "at these altars, / warm shrines— / wash-
ing machines, dryers / with their incense / of men and infants—
/ priestess / or sacrifice?" Over these uneasy and sometimes
querulous sketches, the question hangs unanswered.

Boland's scenes from a marriage are less ambivalent. As presented in these pages, marriage is neither a source of joy nor a cause for complaint. It is a stable partnership, a communion of selves, an intersection of realism and romance:

> The radio is playing downstairs in the kitchen.
> The clock says eight and the light says
> winter. You are pulling up your hood against a bad morning.
>
> Don't leave, I say. Don't go without telling me
> the name of that song. You call it back to me from the stairs:
> "I Wish I Was in Carrickfergus"
>
> and the words open out with emigrant grief the way the streets
> of a small town open out in
> memory: salt-loving fuchsias to one side and
>
> a market in full swing on the other with
> linen for sale and tacky apples and a glass and wire hill
> of spectacles on a metal tray. The front door bangs
>
> and you're gone. I will think of it all morning while a fine
> drizzle closes in, making the distances
> fiction: not of that place but this and of how
>
> restless we would be, you and I, inside the perfect
> music of that basalt and sandstone
> coastal town. We would walk the streets in
>
> the scentless afternoon of a ballad measure,
> longing to be able
> to tell each other that the starched lace and linen of
>
> adult handkerchiefs scraped your face and left your tears
> falling; how the apples were mush inside the crisp sugar
> shell and the spectacles out of focus.
>
> ("Distances")

Separate but sympathetic, undeceived but open to romance, the players in this drama share a hunger for the actual: for the reality of the town idealized in the sentimental ballad. Here as elsewhere, Boland's luminous details create a vivid scene, while sustaining a tone of equanimity. Two other poems in *Outside History* ("A Different Light"; "Domestic Interior") achieve similar effects, the first presenting the married couple as a "neighborhood on the verge of definition" and the second depicting a loving union, whose "home is a sleeping child, / an open mind / and our effects, / shrugged and settled / in the sort of light / jugs and kettles / grow important by."

And what role do real children play in this poetic vision? Boland's delicacy of feeling is nowhere more apparent than in her poems about motherhood, which ardently embrace the maternal role. "Sarah on Holiday" recalls a vacation in the West of Ireland, where the poet-mother puts out a "superstitious feast of / wheat biscuits, apples, / orange juice . . ." for her five-year-old daughter. "In the Garden" broods on her daughter's innocence and her own desire to "show [her] things: / how the poplar root / is pushing through, / how your apple tree is doing, / how daisies / shut like traps." And, most poignantly, "Fruit on a Straight-Sided Tray," having reflected on the spatial relationships of objects on a tray, and having argued that "the true subject is the space between them," discovers its own true subject in its closing lines:

> This is the geometry of the visible, physical tryst
> between substances, disguising for a while the equation
> that kills: you are my child and between us are
>
> spaces, distances. Growing to infinities.

What began as aesthetic meditation ends as an expression of parental loss.

Motherhood is integral to Boland's vision, but her exploration of maternal feeling is only part of a larger effort to discover her identity as an Irish woman and to speak for those women, past and present, whose experience has been excluded from English and Irish poetry. By identifying with other women's lives, she would define her own; and by taking the part of mute inglorious women, she would articulate what she has called "the silences"—the unexpressed lives of other women. In so doing, she would also widen the "human canon":

> When [a woman writer] looks at what has been written by men . . . she is looking at what is *in* the literature. The greater value for women as writers may be their need to be conscious of what is *outside* literature; not just what laps at the shores of that literature, but what that literature could not afford to let in . . . The moment has come when we can look at the experience of women as metaphor of something else, as metaphor for a great deal of troubling and unsettling areas of human experience which have always been a counterweight to the literary tradition and which literature has been skittish about letting in. A lot of that experience is not glamorous or tragic in any sense. It is the experience of the silent and futile and the absurd and the pointless—at least on the surface—routines and rigors of lives. I think we have to retain them as a theme.
>
> (Irish Literary Supplement, Fall 1988)

Women, Boland goes on to say, are "the voice without which the theme would be lost . . . We have to take that great theme, that silence, and commend it as a human theme."

It may be wondered whether modern poetry has really been so exclusive as Boland suggests, and whether the unglamorous routines and rigors of daily lives have not been amply limned in the poems of Robert Frost, R.S. Thomas, Philip Larkin, and more recently, Stephen Dunn, to name only a few. But in its broad outlines Boland's program is plausible, and it is admirably consistent with her practice. In "The Women" she envisions stratified female roles:

> women of work, of leisure, of the night,
> in stove-colored silks, in lace, in nothing,
> with crewel needles, with books, with wide-open legs . . .

before returning to her own role and her own environs, "a hot terrain of linen from the iron, / folded in and over, stacked high, / neatened flat, stoving heat and white." In "Mise Eire" she becomes, in one stanza, a consort of British soldiers ("a sloven's mix / of silk at the wrists, / a sort of dove-strut / in the precincts of the garrison—") and, in another, an emigrant woman "holding her half-dead baby to her / as the wind shifts east / and north over the dirty / water of the wharf." In "The Journey," a wrenching narrative poem, she accompanies Sappho on a tour of the underworld, where she encounters the ghastly sight of women cradling and nursing infants who have died of childhood illnesses:

> Then to my horror I could see to each
> nipple some had clipped a limpet shape—
> suckling darknesses—while others had their arms
> weighed down, making terrible pietas.

Sappho warns her not to distance herself from these women or define them by their social roles:

> She took my sleeve and said to me "be careful.
> Do not define these women by their work:
> not as washerwomen trussed in dust and sweating,
> muscling water into linen by the river's edge
>
> "nor as court ladies brailled in silk
> on wool, and woven with an ivory unicorn
> and hung, nor as laundresses tossing cotton,
> brisking daylight with lavender and gossip.
>
> "But these are women who went out like you
> when dusk became a dark sweet with leaves,
> recovering the day, stooping, picking up
> teddy bears and rag dolls and tricycles and buckets . . .

Dissolving social and historical distinctions, Boland speaks eloquently for any mother—any parent—who has lost a child.

Or rather, she tries to speak. She attempts to utter the unutter-
able. For, as Sappho admonishes her, "what you have seen is
beyond speech, / beyond song, only not beyond love. . ." To
devote one's art to the articulation of silences is to place great
faith in the power of language, both as a tool of consciousness
and as an agent of redemption. But if Boland's art, as a whole,
affirms that faith, her poems also contain their own subversive
nemesis, their own critique. Like many modern poets Boland
worships at the altar of language while lamenting the failings of
her god. "What We Lost," a poem about the oral tradition, regrets
the loss of unwritten stories handed down through generations of
women. "The Oral Tradition" recalls the story, overheard after a
reading, of a woman who gave birth in an open meadow, her
undocumented experience taking its place in legend and song:

> she lay down
> in vetch and linen
> and lifted up her son
> to the archive
> they would shelter in:
>
> the oral song
> avid as superstition
> layered like amber in
> the wreck of a language
> and the remnants of a nation.

And "Fever," a moving reconstruction of her grandmother's
death, imagines the inarticulate suffering, the "soaked-through
midnights" and "histories I never learned / to predict the lyric
of," while arguing that "what we lost is a contagion / that breaks
out in what cannot be / shaken out from words or beaten out /
from meaning . . ." In each of these poems Boland attempts to
articulate the "history of silences," while acknowledging the fail-
ures of language.

In "The Serinette Principle: The Lyric in Contemporary Poetry" (*Parnassus*, v. 15, n. 2, pp. 7–25) Boland speaks of "going back to the source of the lyric" and of "our obligation and our gift, as human beings, to feel our way back into words." And in "The Muse Mother," having observed a mother tending to her child, she hopes that such examples might teach her "a new language: / to be a sibyl, / able to sing the past / in pure syllables, / limning hymns sung / to belly wheat or a woman / able to speak at last / my mother tongue." Those twin aims are laudable, and to the first, Boland seems particularly well suited. In her best poems she demonstrates a gift for "feeling [her] way back into words":

> I turn a switch and the garden grows.
> A whole summer's work in one instant!
> I press my face to the glass. I can see
> shadows of lilac, of fuchsia; a dark likeness of blackcurrant:
>
> little clients of suddenness, how sullen they are at
> the margins of the light.
> They need no rain, they have no roots.
> I reach out a hand; they are gone.
>
> ("Midnight Flowers")

Whether Boland will also create a new language or even a highly original style remains to be seen. William Logan has characterized Boland as a master of fashionable idioms: the "incident reminiscent, its tone the retrospect melancholy, its diction the vernacular significant" (*New York Times Book Review*, 21 April 1991). And in her weaker moments Boland does sound less like herself than like the voices she admires. Coming upon the lines

> working a nappy liner
> over his sticky, loud
> round of a mouth

one hears the adjectival voice of Elizabeth Bishop, channeled, as it were, through the medium of Seamus Heaney. The subject has certainly changed, but the language has some distance to go.

Yet if any Irish woman can extend the language, or make herself heard in Ireland, where male voices still prevail in the anthologies as well as the pubs, it is probably Eavan Boland. She possesses formidable verbal resources, among them a gift of phrasing and a feel for texture:

> and children still bramble-height
> and fretful from the heat and a final
> brightness stickle-backing that particular
>
> patch of grass across which light
> was short-lived and elegiac . . .
> ("We Are Human History, We Are Not Natural History")

This is dense, intricate, and felicitous. It represents, in small, Boland's visual and auditory gifts, her balance of intellect and feeling, her commendable extension of "the human canon."

1991

The Art of Mary Beckett

TOWARD THE END of Mary Beckett's story "The Pursuit of Happiness," a young woman named Josephine, who has suffered a heartbreak, looks out through parted curtains at a rainy night. As the light from her living room streaks the wet asphalt, the rain in turn disturbs the light, causing it to shift and shimmer. Watching the play of light and water, Josephine realizes that she has "mistaken the order of things. It was not that the rain disturbed the light but the light that tortured the rain. She had it then in the power of a jerk of her wrist to cut off the light, and in the dark the rain would slip easily, steadily, into the receptive earth." On an impulse, Josephine whirls back the wine-velvet curtain, "so that the whole stretch of the road was laid open with the flashing blade of a curved sword."

In its immediacy, its quiet drama, and its assertion of personal freedom within an ethos of confinement, that moment typifies the vision of Mary Beckett, whose abiding theme is the survival of the spirit within circumstances that would diminish or destroy it. Since 1980, Mary Beckett has explored that theme in three noteworthy books, and over the past decade she has become an important voice in contemporary Irish letters. Born in Belfast in 1926, Beckett began writing stories at the age of twenty-three, originally for BBC radio and later for literary magazines in Belfast, Cork, and Dublin. After her marriage in 1956 she stopped writing for twenty years, setting aside her literary work to rear her five children. In 1980, *A Belfast Woman*, her first collection of stories, earned her national attention. In 1987 her novel *Give Them Stones* appeared to considerable acclaim, Colm Tóibín calling it "the best novel written about the North over the past twenty years." Her most recent book is *A Literary Woman* (1990), a collection of ten finely wrought, closely integrated stories set in suburban Dublin. In his review for the *Irish News*, Ciaran McKeown predicted that the collection would "take its place with the very best in the high tradition of Irish short stories."

Brian Moore has called Mary Beckett "an extraordinary miniaturist of ordinary lives," and while that description does not quite do justice to her achievement, it does identify her chosen genre and her dominant subject. For the most part, Beckett's stories are short, linear, and void of high drama. With few exceptions, her protagonists are restless, capable women leading straitened lives. Circumscribed by hardship and constrained by repressive social environments, her characters struggle to get by, emotionally as well as financially. Although her stories sometimes end in Joycean epiphanies, their prevailing ambience is more often social than solitary; and though their moods are sometimes poetic, their settings are the stuff of common prose. Densely textured and infused with quotidian detail, Beckett's stories exemplify the quality Patricia Hampl attributes to the diaries of Anne Frank: "an extraordinary commitment to the immediacy of individual experience in the face of crushing circumstances" (*New York Times Book Review*, March 5, 1995, p. 1). But if Beckett's dominant theme is personal integrity, and if her intent is to explore the negotiations of the private self with spouses, families, societal constraints, and violent political realities, her explorations of the private life are a far cry from the essays of Virginia Woolf or the diaries of Anaïs Nin. "It was a bleak grey day," writes Beckett in "A Farm of Land," but the sun broke through for a moment and lit the lime tree on the breast of the rise so that every branch and twig glowed with a springing life." At such moments Beckett honors private experience, recording a moment of bright release within the "dark enclosed days." But in the world portrayed by Beckett, there is scant leisure for the cultivation of sensibility or the analysis of delicate feelings. Moments of introspection are few, and "moments of being" even fewer.

Mary Beckett grew up in Belfast in a family of teachers, and she herself taught school in Ardoyne until the age of thirty, when she married and moved to Dublin. Some of the stories in her first collection were written while she was still living in Belfast, and all are set in her native city. In its depiction of ordinary lives, its concentration on a single Irish city, its naturalistic exactitude, and its limning of emotional constriction, *A Belfast Woman* invites comparisons with Joyce's *Dubliners*. But that first impression is somewhat wide of the mark, and it cannot survive a close reading of the stories. Where Joyce employs analysis and judgment, Beckett's way is intuitive and empathic. Where Joyce uses Little Chandler, Eveline, Gabriel Conroy and the others to illustrate spiritual "paralysis" and to express his critical disdain, Beckett tends rather to listen to her characters' stories, taking a forgiving if also realistic attitude. And where Joyce's characters are often passive victims, Beckett's are usually quite the opposite. Embedded though they are in the social and political matrix of Northern Ireland, they push firmly against societal constraints. As often as not, they define themselves against—rather than within—the social norms.

That is not to say that Beckett's characters are rebels or romantic isolates, bohemians or artists. Most often they are wives, mothers, nieces, and daughters, who for reasons of conscience find themselves at odds with common expectation. In "Theresa," a story exploring racial tensions, a young woman impregnated by a black American serviceman elects to keep and rear the child, marrying a compliant Irish suitor and settling in her own neighborhood. The child herself grows into a robust, self-assertive person.

In "A Farm of Land," a woman with no love of farming and no tolerance for its brutality chooses to sell her parents' farm after their death, moving herself and her sons to Belfast. Her choice, however conscientious, violates custom and tradition. In "Ruth," a mother rears her daughter's illegitimate child after the daughter's untimely death. The mother's trangression is not so much that she sanctions pregnancy out of wedlock as that she speaks so openly of her feelings, rejecting the emotional repression that is the norm. "That's what's wrong with us all," she tells the two local gossips who pay her a visit. "But wouldn't it have eased him, too," she says of her late husband, "if he'd talked and not been so stern with himself always?" The gossips listen, but once out of earshot they condemn their neighbor for her openness—and, ironically, for not providing the information they came for. "A lot of snash and blathers," says the meaner one, "and not a word but what's been common property for years . . . Did we hear where Ruth's gone?"

The assertion of personal independence, so evident in Beckett's domestic dramas, assumes center stage in her treatments of sectarian conflict. One of her most moving stories, "Flags and Emblems," pits a wife's emotional needs against the political allegiances of her husband, a nationalist who has spent his evenings at sectarian meetings, neglecting his wife and marriage. In retaliation his wife puts a Union Jack in the hand of their child, who displays it during a royal visit. For the husband the results are catastrophic, and his wife deeply regrets her impulsive action. "She realized that she had impaled him, not for one afternoon but in a small town hoarding memories, for the length of his life." Yet in the end, wife and husband reconcile, and politics recede before the force of conjugal love: "He stroked her head as it leaned there and swiftly the wealth that had almost disintegrated in despair through his neglect came to warm stirring life in his arms."

If "Flags and Emblems" is the most poignant of the sectarian stories, "A Belfast Woman" is the most ambitious. In this tale of courage and tenacity, Beckett sets the decency and humanity of Mary Harrison, a middle-aged Catholic widow, against the violence and intolerance of those who threaten to burn her out. Mary Harrison's deceased husband, whose lineage was Protestant, "felt so ashamed when the Protestants did something nasty," and she herself feels "disgraced" by the violence of the I.R.A. Yet, though she is appalled by the shootings and bombings, Mary Harrison is no activist or rebel. She is a private citizen caught in the crossfire —and a spokesperson for others like herself. "It's not right," she reminds us, "to put the blame on poor powerless people. The most of us never did anything but stay quiet and put up with things the way they were. And we never taught our children to hate the others nor filled their heads with their wrongs the way it's said we did."

Beckett's title story is one of three in *A Belfast Woman* to be told in the first person, and the force of the story derives, in part, from the quiet vehemence of its narrative voice. In her novel *Give Them Stones*, published seven years later, Beckett again employs the first-person viewpoint and the personal voice to considerable advantage; and again the main character is a woman caught in sectarian warfare. *Give Them Stones* chronicles the life of Martha Murtagh, a wife and mother who gains financial independence by establishing her own home bakery in a Catholic district of Belfast. Earthy, canny, and compassionate, she is also independent in her opinions—and in her treatment of national icons:

> Then he lent me his book of Yeats plays and I read them over and over again. I didn't think much of Cuchulain. I didn't believe all this 'honour' stuff that made him kill his friend and then his own son. I didn't like the way he treated Emer, his wife, and I was sorry my wee godchild was called after her even though I liked the sound of the name. I didn't say that to them, and of course I didn't say it to anybody else because I would have had to explain too much.

Despite her disbelief in "honour" Martha Murtagh supports the nationalist cause and the Irish Republican Army, until she witnesses the double-kneecapping of a teenaged boy. Having earlier reaped the wrath of British soldiers by banning them from her bakery, she now condemns the I.R.A. for their brutality and refuses to pay them protection money. In retribution the I.R.A. burns down her bakery and her husband's family home.

In *Give Them Stones* Mary Beckett interweaves the personal ordeals of Martha Murtagh with the social fabric and the public events of the early seventies—the civil rights movement, the Falls Road curfew, the first sectarian murders. What gives the novel its uncommon power is not only the inherent drama of the political events but the humane and even-tempered viewpoint of the narrator, whose sanity is a rebuke to political hysteria. Martha Murtagh's circumstances are not unusual for her time and place, but she is herself extraordinary in her ability to maintain her integrity and her balanced realism amidst social disorder.

Martha Murtagh is in fact the unrelenting realist, whether she is speaking of love, marriage, death, or political upheaval. Describing her decision to marry her husband Dermot, a cautious, passive man, she focuses not on the man but his domestic equipment. "There was a gas cooker with four rings and a grill, and below, an oven. Beside it there was a sink with hot and cold chromium taps. I knew then I wanted to marry Dermot." Recounting her response to her grandmother's death, she is similarly candid: "I can't say I mourned my granny much. She was a trouble to herself and to everybody else." Responding to a British officer who demands to know her political allegiance, she is both shrewd and truthful: "'Are you a Republican?' he asked and I shrugged. I was going to be a heroine but instead I said, 'I am a home baker.'" And in her dealings with herself, she is equally realistic, faulting herself for cowardice and resisting the temptations of easy sentiment. At the end of the novel, when she has lost everything but her husband's passionless company, she listens to Dermot declaring that he will do "anything at all" for her, "[a]nything in the world." Her response is characteristic:

> It was not true, of course. He wouldn't even give me any money unless I kept on at him. Maybe he thought it was true, though. At any rate, it was nice to listen to. After all, maybe I don't always face the truth about myself either.

As an extension of "A Belfast Woman" and an exploration of personal independence, *Give Them Stones* looks backward to Beckett's first collection. But in its moments of introspection and its focus on marriage and the family, it looks forward to her most recent fiction. In *A Literary Woman*, political issues recede almost entirely, although one story ("The Bricks Are Fallen Down") is set partially in Belfast. Calmly and steadily, these stories probe the self's internal quarrels, the disappointments of marriage, and the pain of rearing children. For the most part the characters in these later stories enjoy material comforts, but they are no less troubled than those of Beckett's earlier fiction. If anything they are more so, insofar as their troubles originate in the psyche rather than the social fabric.

Yet if *A Literary Woman* has a dominant theme, it is not inner conflict or interpersonal relations but the self's capacity for survival and growth. Facing difficult truths, the characters in these stories correct their courses—or resolve to alter their lives. In "The Long Engagement" a woman liberates herself by breaking off a protracted engagement with a bachelor who has taken her for granted. In "Sudden Infant Death" a mother who has suffered the trauma of losing a child resolves to "work on" her marriage and to treat her husband with greater generosity. In "Under Control" a mother accused by her daughter of being a controlling person examines her conscience and her motives. And in "Inheritance" a career woman who has resisted having children discovers the ferocity of maternal love: "Would this oppression, this anxiety, stay with her all [her son's] life? she wondered. Was this perhaps what love was?"

Of those who learn lessons in *A Literary Woman*, none is more fully chastened than the protagonist of Beckett's title story. Winifred Teeling is not a writer *per se* but the author of malicious, anonymous letters, fashioned to destabilize—if not ruin—the lives of their recipients. In several related stories, her letters cause trouble, both within the family and within the characters' psyches. Although on balance the letters fail of their effects, they do prompt their recipients to examine their lives and to define themselves against unjust appraisals of their actions. And though Beckett portrays her "literary woman" as irretrievably evil, her portrait is not without mercy and understanding. Venemous and perverse, Winifred Teeling is also a friendless loner, who only wants "a bit of excitement, something to happen." And in the end she sees "the foolishness of all those fruitless letters."

To portray a sociopath with compassion is no small challenge, but in "A Literary Woman," as in her fiction generally, Mary Beckett has achieved a rare blend of empathy and objectivity, critical realism and imaginative insight. About fifty years ago, in *The Necessary Angel* (1942), Wallace Stevens lamented the loss of "the idea of nobility" in modern art, attributing that loss to a "failure in the relation between the imagination and reality" and to what he called "the pressure of reality." Nobility, he argued, is a "violence from within that protects us from a violence without. It is the imagination pressing back against the pressure of reality." The author of "The Auroras of Autumn" is hardly to be likened to the author of *Give Them Stones*, but to read Beckett's fiction is to be reminded of Stevens's formulation. For in the work of this exemplary Irish realist, ideas of nobility are tested and redefined, and a "violence from without" confronts a keen and mature imagination.

1995

Hardness and Softness[1]

IN ONE OF his many essays on the Irish character, Sean O' Faolain posits a connection between the inherent kindness of the Irish people and the brutality of rural Irish life:

> You cannot scan this Irish line without . . . referring constantly to its basic rhythm of delicacy of feeling—that extraordinary sensibility to human feeling for which we Irish are at once notorious and famous, loved and despised, our well-known desire to please. . . . Hardness as the father of softness. We shall never know what we owe to the wet sack on the shoulders, the dunging cow, the steam from the frieze pants before the fire.
>
> (*The Bell*, Vol. XI, No. 2, November, 1945, p. 652)

O' Faolain goes on to observe that the "peasant kindness" he attributes to the Irish is "always indiscriminate, often frightening, and frequently disgusting. The slaverings at Irish funerals are a hideous invasion of human privacy."

O' Faolain's remarks were written some fifty years ago, but they bear directly on the stories of John McGahern, where brutal fact and delicate feeling exist in close proximity, and where a sternly realistic outlook finds expression in a gentle, tentative style. Whether his setting has been a Dublin pub, or an English

---

[1]John McGahern. *The Collected Stories*. London: Faber and Faber, 1992.

construction site, or, most often, the rural community in Co. Leitrim where he lives and works, McGahern has written with clarity and objectivity, making few concessions to nationalist or religious pieties and fewer still to easy sentiment. Yet if his stance has been that of the seasoned realist, his manner has often been otherwise. Diffident and tentative, his prose has a softness that belies its content and a subtlety of feeling that sorts strangely with brute realities. Addressing his three abiding subjects—the life of the parish; the dynamics of the family; the growth and death of intimate relationships—he has explored a tonal range that is difficult to define but can be heard—and felt—on nearly every page. Its most prominent element is a weary pessimism, a certainty of "life's eventual hopelessness," brightened by glimpses of remembered happiness. In McGahern's stories, joys and sorrows come and go. What stays is an ethos of desolation.

McGahern's dark vision may be, in part, an expression of temperament, but it is also the distillation of difficult experience. Born in 1934 and reared in Counties Leitrim and Roscommon, McGahern rode to Mass on a sidecar and can remember children bringing turf to the school where his mother taught. When he writes of the "drudge of life from morning to night to feed the mouths . . . The ugly and skin shapes of starlings, beaks voracious at the rim of the nest, days grown heavier with the burden of the carrying," his recollections have the ring of earned authority. When McGahern was still very young, his mother died, and he went to live in the barracks at Cootehall, where his father was stationed. If one may judge from his fiction, it was not a nurturing environment, but he was fortunate enough to be befriended by a Protestant family, whom he remembers with affection. In their house he read Scott, Dickens, and Zane Grey, and othewise nourished his literary sensibilties.

By late adolescence McGahern had decided to become a national teacher. That plan was scrapped after a few months at St. Patrick's Training College in Drumcondra, where he found both students and teachers sadistic, the boys from the Gaeltacht being the worst of all. Subsequently, he earned a degree from University College, Dublin, and after a period of doing manual labor in England, he took a job at a Christian Brothers School in Drogheda. Finding the school's atmosphere closed and repressive, he moved to Dublin, where he wrote his first novel and enjoyed the cultural life of the capital city. When his novel *The Barracks* (1962) won him a Macauley Fellowship, he embarked on a period of European travel, visiting Germany, Finland, and Spain and continuing to work on his next novel. When *The Dark* appeared in 1965, it was banned in his home country; and when McGahern returned to Ireland, he discovered that he had been fired from his teaching position at the St. John the Baptist School in Clontarf, ostensibly for marrying a foreign woman. The order had come directly from Archbishop John McQuaid. For the next five years McGahern lived and wrote in Paris, London, Barcelona, the United States, and England, but in 1970, having remarried, he bought a piece of land in County Leitrim between the villages of Mohill and Ballinamore. In 1974 he went to live there with his wife Madeline, and he has remained there ever since, at once a native and a widely-traveled observer of local custom. By his own account he is "a rotten farmer."[2]

McGahern's personal history is not unique in Ireland, whose literary exiles have oftentimes come home. What is unusual is his return, not only to Ireland but to the scenes of his childhood and the confines of a provincial Catholic community. McGahern's life-choices have situated him in the roles of both outsider and insider, intimate with his subjects by virtue of birth and upbringing but separate by virtue of travel and education. Nor is his situation precisely comparable to that of the Protestant, Anglo-Irish writers—Yeats, Shaw, Synge, *et.al.*—who found themselves, like

---

[2]See "Out of the Dark: A Profile of John McGahern," in Colm Tóibín, *The Trial of the Generals*. (Dublin: Raven Arts Press, 1990), pp. 94–102.

Louis MacNeice, "banned from the candles of the Irish poor." Rotten farmer or not, McGahern's rapport with the hills and fields is nearly as close as Patrick Kavanagh's; and despite his collisions with the puritanical elements of Irish Catholicism, his portrayal of priests and devotees is not unsympathetic. Like the poet John Montague, whose situation resembles his own, McGahern combines an internationalist's outlook with a native's knowledge of local history. If the first is evident in his reflections on social change, the second can be felt in the dense, plain particulars of his prose.

No one is more aware than McGahern of the transitional character and the instability of postwar Irish society. McGahern has written five acclaimed novels, but in a conversation with the journalist and novelist Colm Tóibín, he lamented the lack of a tradition of the novel in Ireland and the absence of a fixed, settled society on which a novelist might feed.[3] And in "Oldfashioned," his panoramic, elegiac story about the befriending of a Catholic boy by a retired Protestant couple, he appraises the changes that have transformed the Irish countryside. Among the most salient are the replacement of horses, carts, and traps by tractors, cars, and lorries; the migration of young people from the farms to Dublin; the displacement of the parish priest by the local politician; the democratization of the Church after Vatican II; and the invasion of color television, which creates a "strange living light" in nearly every rural home, a glow "more widespread than the little red lamps before the pictures of the Sacred Heart years before."

Yet if the social fabric of Ireland as a whole is unstable and increasingly secular, the Irish parish as depicted by McGahern remains a coherent social unit, its agrarian rhythms resistant to fashion, its customs and values rooted firmly in the nineteenth century. "They're all driving around in cars," observes a Cavan

---

[3] Tóibín, p. 101.

policeman in "The Creamery Manager," "but the mentality is still of the jennet and cart." And to those who remain in it—or return to it—the parish offers stability and succor, especially in time of grief and mourning. Of the many stories which dramatize the social cohesion of the parish, the most memorable is "Faith, Hope, and Charity," which explores the impact of sudden death on a small farming community. When the son of a local family is killed on a construction site in England, the family spends money it doesn't have to bring the body home for burial. Aware of the family's straitened circumstances, their neighbors organize a dance to pay the funeral expenses. The music is supplied by Faith, Hope, and Charity, a band of three elderly bachelor brothers who play the fiddle, drums, and accordion, respectively, and perform "for a few crates of stout." Poignant, mellow, and serio-comic, "Faith, Hope, and Charity" celebrates the nurturant coherence of the Irish parish and the streak of kindness in the Irish character.

Not all of McGahern's portraits are so affectionate, and not all of his parishioners are so kind. If the parish can be supportive, it can also be hidebound, claustrophobic, vindictive, and cruel. One vivid instance of cruelty occurs in "Eddie Mac," the tale of a roguish football hero. When Eddie Mac suffers a knee injury and can no longer please his fans, he finds himself "taunted and jeered every time he went near the ball by the same people that had chaired him shoulder high from the field the year before." Parochial cruelty erupts again in "A Slip-Up," where the misfortunes of a local farmer provide entertainment for the regulars at the pub:

> All the people were elated too on the small farms around the lakes for weeks after Fraser Woods had tried to hang himself from a branch of an apple tree in his garden, the unconcealed excitement in their voices as they said, "Isn't it terrible what happened to poor Fraser?" and the lust on their faces as they waited for their excitement to be mirrored.

And in "Christmas," one of McGahern's harshest stories, a drunken policeman attending midnight Mass demolishes the facades of piety, respectability, and goodwill. Loudly denouncing his neighbors for their lust and selfishness, he singles out the tax collector, "the biggest hypocrite in the parish," for special condemnation.

Although McGahern's stance is often that of social critic, he is seldom so caustic as his drunken *garda*. Nor does the generosity of "Faith, Hope, and Charity" strike his dominant note. The prevailing tone is a blend of judgment and mercy, forgiveness and critical asperity. Nowhere is that tone more evident than in "Swallows," a tale of lost hopes and abandoned aspirations. The protagonist is an aging police sergeant who encounters a promising younger man in the course of duty. The younger man, a Dublin surveyor, is also an accomplished violinist, who owns a priceless instrument acquired in Avignon. After hearing the young man play, and after learning that the surveyor is on his way to perform in Galway, the sergeant expresses his admiration and bids him a safe journey. Alone with his whiskey and his housekeeper Biddy, he falls into a revery, in which he contrasts the romantic world of the younger man with his own provincial environs:

> Tonight in Galway, in a long dress of burgundy velvet, satin in her hair, the delicate white hands of Eileen O'Neill would flicker on the white keyboard as the Surveyor played, while Mrs. Killboy would say to him at the CWA, "Something will have to be done about Jackson's thieving ass, Sergeant, it'll take the law to bring him back to his senses, nothing less, and those thistles of his will be blowing again over the townland this year with him dead drunk in the pub, and is Biddy's hens laying at all this weather, mine have gone on unholy strike, and I hear you were measuring the road today, you and a young whipper-snapper from Dublin, not even the guards can do anything unknownst in this place . . .

Refraining from overt discursive judgment, McGahern juxtaposes images of high culture with those of thieving donkeys and reluctant hens. The contrast speaks for itself, evoking both the colorful familiarity and the sad provinciality of the Sergeant's social environment. That he once played the fiddle himself at local dances only heightens the pathos and irony of his revery.

Bittersweet ironies permeate McGahern's treatments of the Irish parish. At his lighter moments, one is reminded less of Joyce or Frank O'Connor than of Garrison Keillor. To turn from McGahern's vision of the parish to his view of the family, however, is to encounter a more astringent vision and a less benevolent attitude. With few exceptions McGahern's images of the family are hard and cold, and his themes are those of the embittered heart. As portrayed by McGahern, the Irish family is less a nurturing source than a binding institution. Patriarchal and repressive, it constricts its members while they are at home and trammels them long after they've moved away. At its worst it exploits them and diminishes their chances for happiness in adult life.

McGahern's family scenes are seldom heartening, but the most appalling can be found in "Korea," one of his earlier stories. In this tale of ruthless survival, a disillusioned veteran of the Anglo-Irish War, who witnessed the executions of a sixteen-year-old boy and a man in his early thirties, urges his son to go to America and offers to pay the fare. Not long afterward, the son discovers his father's ulterior motive. Once in America, the boy will be conscripted for service in the Korean War. The family will receive two hundred and fifty dollars a month while he serves—and ten thousand dollars if he is killed. Overhearing his father speak of his potential benefits, the boy realizes that his "youth [has] ended." Yet in the evening, after he's flatly refused his father's offer, he feels closer than ever to the man who would send him off to kill or be killed. Watching his father's every movement, he feels "as if [he] too had to prepare [him]self to murder."

The cold exploitation dramatized in "Korea" has a milder counterpart in "Sierra Leone," where another manipulative father attempts to reorder his economic affairs. In this instance the father calls his grown son home from Dublin in hopes of making a secret deal. Fearful that after his death his hated in-laws will take over the farm, the father offers to transfer ownership to his son, thereby disinheriting his wife. Without so much as entertaining the proposal, the son refuses. But his going home, however fruitless and dispiriting, has serious personal consequences. To answer his father's summons he had to cancel a planned weekend with his lover at a tenuous point in their relationship. As things turn out, his choice proves pivotal.

Yet another instance of paternal malice occurs in "The Gold Watch," one of McGahern's finest stories. Once again a father's aggression impinges on a son's adult relationship, though in this instance the relationship rests on a surer footing. When the son, a Dublin civil servant, brings his fiancée home for the first time, his father insults her, and the couple leave the following morning. After a later visit to the family home, the son brings back his father's gold watch, which had been broken accidentally by his mother and had become the focus of a bitter quarrel. As a wedding present, the young man's fiancée has the watch repaired and restored. He, in turn, buys a modern watch for his father, who overtly accepts it but covertly endeavors to destroy it. After repeatedly abusing the watch, he suspends it in a barrel of blue poison, where his son later discovers it. A bitter confirmation of his father's hatred, that discovery prompts a moment of introspection:

> I stood in that moonlit silence as if waiting for some word or truth, but none came, none ever came; and I grew amused at that part of myself that still expected something, standing like a fool out there in all the moonlit silence, when only what *was* increased or diminished as it changed, became only what is, becoming again what *was* even faster than the small second hand endlessly circling in the poison.

Elevated in tone but personal in content, these reflections both reveal and conceal a primal hurt. Shunting experience into the past—into "what *was*"—they ward off the pain of the present moment.

A sense of primal hurt pervades the family situations in McGahern's stories. At best his characters experience their family ties as constraints, or habitual obligations, or empty pieties. At worst they experience them as crippling burdens and poisonous social environments. Although McGahern himself grew up in a family of seven, where he was the eldest child, his family scenes are void of festivities or dinners or family outings. They focus on one-to-one encounters, most often acrimonious confrontations of fathers and sons. "And that phrase from the Bible is true," remarks the narrator in "Gold Watch," reflecting on the death of kindness between himself and his father. "[A]fter enough suffering a kind of iron enters the soul." In McGahern's vision of the family, iron is the dominant element, though in the later stories (particularly "Bank Holiday" and "A Country Funeral"), anger is tempered by compassion. Apart from happiness, what is most conspicuously missing is the softening influence of a maternal presence. Mothers are peripheral and ineffectual. And in "A Country Funeral" the mother herself has iron in her soul. When she speaks to her sons, her voice has "a sudden frailty" which "only serve[s] to point up the different shades of its steel."

Fierce and free of sentimentality, McGahern's view of the Irish family is also less than comprehensive. To this reader it seems both narrow and one-sided. But if the sins of the family bring out the bitter critic in McGahern, the travails of love bring out another side entirely. They disclose the chastened idealist, the melancholy amorist:

> When he was young he had desired too much, and so spread his own fear. Now that he was close to losing everything—was in the direct path of the wind—it was little short of amazing that he should come on this extraordinary breathing space.
>
> ("Bank Holiday")

These sentences describe a fifty-year-old civil servant who has fallen in love with a young American woman. Far from disillusioned, McGahern's tone is undeceived but receptive, disabused but open to the miraculous.

That complex of feelings recurs often in McGahern's portrayals of intimate relationships. He is at once the realist and the wary romantic. In McGahern's stories the women are nearly always "beautiful," or almost beautiful, and their suitors waste no time in telling them so. Relationships themselves are portrayed as tender, faltering, fragile, and mysterious. "Who knows the person another will find their happiness or unhappiness with?" asks the narrator of "Sierra Leone." Yet if relationships are ethereal and ineffable, they are also grounded in history. They arise from the particulars of time and place. "Sierra Leone" chronicles an illicit love affair that begins during the Cuban Missile Crisis, "in the freedom of the fear." It ends when the young woman's other lover, a politician in his early fifties, accepts the offer of a lucrative job in Sierra Leone, and the young woman decides to go with him. Not unrelated to the outcome of the affair is the fact that Ireland "as a small nation with a history of oppression was suddenly becoming useful in the Third World."

Yet though historical circumstances play a role in this and other stories (particularly "The Conversion of William Kirkwood," where a middle-aged scion of the crumbling Protestant Ascendancy marries a Catholic woman), the force of history pales in comparison to the influence of the family. "That's the sadness," remarks a barman in "Sierra Leone." "You don't know whether to look after them or your own life." Just such a conflict drives both "Sierra Leone" and "Gold Watch," determining structure as well as theme. McGahern usually opts for the linear plot, but in those and other stories he employs an intricate, contrapuntal structure. A story of a troubled family, set in the country, runs parallel to a love story, set in Dublin. Intersecting and interweaving, the two patterns progress to a common resolution. In these stories, as in his magisterial fifth novel, *Amongst Women* (1990), the Irish family continues to shape, if not to rule, the lives of the urban professionals who have long since moved away. "I visited my parents until they died," explains the narrator of "Bank Holiday" to his American lover. And when his mother, the second to die, is laid in her grave, he feels "almost glad. The natural wind now blew directly on him."

Were history and family the primary determinants in intimate relationships, and were the characters themselves not responsible for what happens, McGahern's stories would be less engaging than they are. As John Gardner remarks in *The Art of Fiction*, "the writer who denies that human beings have free will . . . is one who can write nothing of interest." As it happens, in his many stories about broken relationships ("Parachutes," "Doorways," "All Sorts of Impossible Things," "Peaches," "My Love, My Umbrella," "Sierra Leone," "Along the Edges") personal choice is not merely integral in determining outcomes; it is crucial and irreversible. The sad schoolteacher James Sharkey in "All Sorts of Impossible Things" gives his girlfriend an ultimatum: "Will you marry me or not?" When she declines to answer, he abruptly rejects her:

> "Goodbye, then." He steeled himself to turn away.
> Twice he almost paused, but no voice calling him back came. At the open iron gate above the stream he did pause. "If I cross it here it is the end. Anything is better than the anguish of uncertainty. If I cross here I cannot turn back even if she should want." He counted till ten and looked back, but her back was turned, walking slowly uphill to the house. As she passed through the gate he felt a tearing that broke as an inaudible cry.

This scene shares the melodrama, if not the mortal outcome, of the ballad "Úna Bhán," where another lover makes a fatal crossing and commits a fatal error. Though usually portrayed with greater subtlety, such choices doom most of the intimate relationships in McGahern's stories—and are regretted ever after. In "My Love, My Umbrella," a young man tires of his lover and abandons her. In "Doorways," the narrator declines to offer support at a critical point—and pays the price. In "Peaches," a married man fails to defend his wife when she is sexually accosted, and their already smoldering marriage goes up in smoke. So persistent is this pattern, it comes as a surprise when, in "Bank Holiday," a relationship continues into the future, despite the male character's doubts and fears. The more usual outcome is a sharp, guilt-ridden sense of regret:

> There had been that moment too that might have been grasped, and had not, and love had died—she had admitted as much. It would have led on to what? To happiness, for a while, or the absence of this present sense of loss, or to some other sense of loss . . .
>
> ("Along the Edges")

Plaintive and remorseful, this could speak for most of the relationships in McGahern's stories. Failure is not the exception but the rule, and those who fail have mainly themselves to blame.

McGahern's laments for lost love grow predictable after a while, and at their weakest they drift into self-pity. But his portrayals of romantic love, like his portrayals of the parish and the family, contribute to a larger and more penetrating vision of human experience—a view of life that is at once intimate and distant, judgmental and forgiving. Like the visions of other Irish realists—Synge, in particular—it takes its bearings from an awareness of impermanence and a sense of incipient loss. And at its core lies a cognizance of mortality, which in McGahern, as in other Irish writers, can seem at times obsessive.

Few writers can surpass McGahern in evoking scenes of remembered happiness, be it the halcyon days of a couple in love or a youthful bachelor's nights on the town:

> There was extraordinary peace and loveliness in those first weeks together that I will always link with those high-ceilinged rooms—the eager rush of excitement I felt as I left the office at

the end of the day; the lingering in the streets to buy some offering of flowers or fruit or wine or bowl and, once, one copper pan; and then rushing up the stairs to call her name . . .

("Gold Watch")

Now he could hardly remember a sentence from those hundreds of evenings. What he did remember was a barman's face, white hair drawn over baldness, an avid follower of Christy Ring; a clock, a spiral iron staircase to the Gents, the cold of marble on the wristbone, footsteps passing outside in summer, the sound of heavy rain falling before closing time.

("Bank Holiday")

Yet what gives such scenes their poignancy, here as elsewhere, is their inherent transience. However radiant, the characters' happiness is always precarious. The curtain is always about to fall.

"How dark is the end of all of life," observes the schoolteacher John in "A Country Funeral"—the last and longest story in McGahern's collection. Of the thirty-four stories it is the most ambitious, and its multiple perspectives on the family, the parish, and the fact of mortality create a structure commensurate with McGahern's complex vision. With overtones of the Biblical and the archetypal, "A Country Funeral" narrates the reluctant return of three urban brothers to their rural origins. For the sake of appearances they agree to attend a hated uncle's funeral in remote Gloria Bog, where they experienced a painful childhood. As the story unfolds, the brothers' diverse outlooks define themselves. Fonsie, confined to a wheelchair, is an inveterate cynic, who vividly recalls his uncle's cruelties and regards rural funeral customs ("the bit of cotton sticking out of the corner of the dead man's mouth") as barbaric and obscene. John, the pale schoolteacher, is a "good listener"—a passive, unambitious man, who adopts the stance of neutral observer. Philly is a vain adventurer, a "burly block of exasperation" in Fonsie's eyes, who earns lucrative wages in the oil fields and returns periodically to "make the big splash" and "do the big fellow" in Dublin. Of the three brothers, only Philly is moved by the experience of the funeral—so much so that he resolves, at the end of the story, to return to Gloria Bog, where "people still mean something," and take over the family farm. "Even the fish," he reminds his cynical brother, "go back to where they came from."

"A Country Funeral" may not be McGahern's final statement, but it has the tone and character of a resolution. In contrast to his other stories, which traffic uneasily between the city and the country, the middle-class profession and the family farm, "A Country Funeral" chronicles a homecoming. And in the differing perpectives of the brothers, the contrasting timbres of their voices, McGahern balances and integrates three components of his moral outlook. "His nature was not hard," says the narrator of Philly, the generous brother, who sees in the country funeral an example of charity and kindness. It is his hard-boiled brother Fonsie who reminds Philly that the good neighbors who attended the wake were only availing themselves of a "chance to get out of their bloody houses before they start to eat one another within," and that the priest who spoke so movingly of the Mystery and the Resurrection was "paid to do that and. . . was nearly late." Between those poles of tenderness and toughness, romantic idealism and hard-edged realism, McGahern has defined a view of life that is neither warm nor cold, hard nor soft, but a distinctive synthesis of the two. And underlying both perspectives is the fact of mortality, whose certainty is cause for both compassion and clear-eyed realism.

That fact is given direct expression in "The Wine Breath," the story of a priest who confronts his unconscious fear of death by recalling a winter burial he witnessed as a child. In his memory the line of mourners who climbed the hill to the graveyard in the snow were "bathed in the eternal." Decades later, they remain a haunting presence. The image recurs in "A Country Funeral," as Fonsie watches his uncle's burial:

> Then it was only the coffin itself and the heads of the mourners that could be seen until they were lost in the graveyard evergreens. In spite of his irritation at this useless ceremony, that

seemed only to show some deep love of hardship or enslavement—they'd be hard put to situate a graveyard in a more difficult or inaccessible place except on the very top of a mountain— he found the coffin and the small band of toiling mourners unbearably moving as it made its low stumbling climb up the hill, and this deepened further his irritation and the sense of complete uselessness.

To the priest in "The Wine Breath" the image of toiling mourners is numinous and timeless. To Fonsie it is an unsettling reminder of peasant subjugation and an emblem of life's futility. What is constant is the image itself and its persistence in McGahern's imagination. Coming at the end of his collection, "A Country Funeral" charts a westward movement, not only toward home but toward greater compassion and acceptance of mortality. In those respects it occupies a place similar to that of "The Dead" in *Dubliners*; and in McGahern, as in Joyce, the graveyard plays a climactic role. If there is a crucial difference, it lies in the humane and homely tone of McGahern's image and its intimate connection to his narrators. In contrast to Joyce's desolate graveyard in Oughterard, McGahern's embraces living mourners, whom his narrators know well. Impersonal and universal, his *memento mori* is also personal and parochial. Imbued with a cold finality, it is also gentle and familiar.

1995

Seán O'Faoláin, 1900–1991

In one of Seán O'Faoláin's late stories, entitled "The Human Thing," an expatriate Irish priest must decide whether to grant a Catholic burial to an apostate—a parishioner who sent his wife and children away and lived with his lover for five years. After much vexation, the world-weary priest agrees to perform the funeral. "Did I do right?" he asks the narrator. "You did the human thing, Father," the narrator replies.

It is a characteristic moment—and a characteristic response. Over the course of his long career, Seán O'Faoláin cast a cool but humane eye on church and state, politics and economics, history and religion. His prodigious, wide-ranging *oeuvre* includes biographies of Irish national heroes, a social history of Ireland, literary criticism, novels of provincial life, eloquent polemics, and some of the most hard-headed, poignant, and incisive stories in modern Irish literature. An ironic realist and committed internationalist, he viewed his "old, small, intimate, and much-trodden country" in a global perspective, its shams and delusions in a clear and analytical light. In his biographies of Daniel O'Connell, Hugh O'Neill, and Eamon De Valera, he limned the contradictions of the Irish mind—its mixture of shrewdness and idealism, mendacity and vision. In *Bird Alone*, set in his native Cork, he evoked the pathos of that provincial city, while denouncing its soul-crushing social attitudes. And in the pages of *The Bell*, the journal he founded and edited from 1940–46, he sought to discover the "real Ireland" behind the national myths, to raise standards of taste, and to bring an end to censorship. Recalling Ireland to its ideals, he condemned "this rising middle-class of ours, full of pietism, profits and ignorant bumptiousness."

Yet for all his moral stringency and austere historicism, Seán O'Faoláin never lost sight of "the human thing." "I like cold writing," he insisted. "[W]hen we see a man luxuriating in his own emotions, it corrodes *our* feelings." But in practice his writing was anything but cold. It was remarkably forgiving. "This famous experience of ours," asks one of his characters, "what else is it but the lamentable record of our carefully concealed mistakes?" And throughout his writing, whether his subject is romantic love, Catholicism, or political strife, one finds affection for the flawed and the imperfect, be it the worn junction points of a tramline, or the blundering Irish Republic, or the human heart itself.

"Had she been smarter," he remarks of one of his characters, "she would have realized that pessimists are usually kind. The gay, bubbling over, have no time for the pitiful." Within the tradition of the Irish short story, which he did much to enrich, Seán O'Faoláin found ample time for the pitiful; and if pessimism and disillusionment mark his later writing, so does the spirit of forgiveness. To the often bleak environs of modern fiction, he brought humor, rigor, intelligence, and what the Irish call "nature" —a generosity of spirit and a profound sympathy for human frailties.

1991

The Pressed Melodeon